International Series in Advanced Management Studies

This series is published in cooperation with the Italian Society of Management (SIMA). It is home to books that focus on advanced and cutting-edge management topics that are likely to have significant impacts on and advantages for companies, institutions and other organizations in the business world. The topics reflect various aspects of management – such as business strategy, corporate finance, entrepreneurship, operations, SME, corporate governance, innovation management, marketing, and corporate communication – as applied to all industries, all types of organizations (profit, public or non profit), and all regions of the globe.

This is a SCOPUS indexed book series.

Book selection procedure:

This series follows a single-blind reviewing procedure. Authors interested in publishing a volume are invited to submit their proposal by e-mail to the Editor-in-Chief, Prof. Alberto Pastore: alberto.pastore@uniroma1.it. Authors are requested to supply the following material: structured abstract (and methodology, if appropriate), table of contents, 2 or 3 sample chapters, CV (including a list of previous publications).

Generoso Branca

Virtual Reality, Real Intentions

Consumers' Evaluation of Product Packaging in Immersive Environments

S I
M A
Società Italiana di
MANAGEMENT

Springer

Generoso Branca
Department of Marketing
Bocconi University
Milan, Italy

ISSN 2366-8814 ISSN 2366-8822 (electronic)
International Series in Advanced Management Studies
ISBN 978-3-032-10141-9 ISBN 978-3-032-10142-6 (eBook)
https://doi.org/10.1007/978-3-032-10142-6

This Springer imprint is published by the registered company Springer Nature Switzerland AG
The registered company address is: Gewerbestrasse 11, 6330 Cham, Switzerland

To all those who never stop dreaming.

Foreword

Two mainstreams appear to define contemporary management literature, broadly in line with certain tendencies that became established in the early 2000s. One stream concerns digital technologies relevant to business management and operational processes, frequently combined with efforts to measure their impact. The other stream focuses on the environmental and social sustainability of business strategies, which can no longer be assessed solely in economic terms. This dual orientation has evolved across business studies, resulting in a body of literature that covers a broad spectrum of topics.

Within this research scenario, Generoso Branca's volume adopts an original and sharply focused perspective fitting the scholarly domain of consumer behavior, which constitutes a recognized field of the scientific sector "*Economia e gestione delle imprese*" in Italy. Specifically, he investigates how consumers evaluate packaged products in virtual reality in comparison with physical reality, offering a comparative experimental analysis that bridges a relevant and timely gap in consumer research and managerial practice.

Packaging has increasingly had significant marketing implications for consumers' purchasing decisions. Firms are very attentive to consumer perceptions when deciding how to package and present products in ways that maximize both attractiveness and sustainability. As the volume demonstrates, virtual reality technologies may facilitate the analysis of consumer preferences regarding the structural, haptic, and visual cues of packaging, without resorting to physical prototypes. This, in turn, offers tangible advantages in terms of cost efficiency and environmental impact. Consequently, the research illustrates the possibility of reconciling environmental and economic sustainability objectives, two dimensions that theory and practice often present as being in a trade-off relationship.

The research findings presented here are valuable both for their contribution to a relatively under-researched field and for their managerial implications. Experimental empirical evidence indicates that virtual reality technologies can effectively replace traditional processes for conducting robust product and packaging tests. By enabling the evaluation of a broader range of solutions in a shorter timeframe, immersive technologies prove mainly beneficial during the early phases of product and packaging development, prototyping, and consumer testing, when manipulating packaging cues is essential. These advantages become even more pronounced when shifting from the micro standpoint of the individual firm to the macro, systemic perspective.

The work is notable regarding the evolution of methodologies for analyzing consumer behavior, as it provides a useful example of how well-designed laboratory experiments can overcome limitations of surveys and related approaches. Moreover, demonstrating the robust findings in consumer studies using immersive technologies opens a promising avenue for academic research, where real-world consumption scenarios are not always accessible.

In my view, the primary requirements for research are methodological rigor and intellectual honesty in deriving findings of relevance for scholars and practitioners alike, as well as the ability to identify original avenues of investigation. This volume clarifies the Author's commendable commitment to such aims, from the systematic design of the overarching research framework, comprising three distinct studies, to the meticulous execution of experiments, made possible in part through the faithful reproduction of physical packages to ensure meaningful comparison with virtual evaluations.

Beyond these qualities, evident here and in his other scientific publications, Generoso Branca shows a genuine passion for research, sustained by a persistent dedication to his work. Having known his lively intellectual curiosity since his time as a student, I am confident in his continued advancement in academia, hoping that he will continue to pursue it with the enthusiasm and curiosity he shows today.

Naples, Italy
August 2025

Riccardo Resciniti

Acknowledgements The author would like to acknowledge all those who provided the materials for the experiment: the two expert designers, Mr. Bove and Mr. Quaglia, for the packaging development; Mare Group for the Virtual Reality environment; Grafica Metelliana for the packaging mock-ups.

Competing Interests The author has no competing interests to declare that are relevant to the content of this manuscript.

Contents

About the Author

Generoso Branca is a Post-Doc Researcher in the Department of Marketing at Bocconi University (Italy), and a Fellow in Marketing Management at SDA Bocconi School of Management (Italy), where he is also a member of the Channel & Retail Lab. He received a Ph.D. from the University of Sannio (Italy), with an additional Doctor Europaeus Certificate.

His research interests focus on consumer behavior and sustainability, diversity and inclusion in the marketplace, and immersive technologies.

Alongside his research activities, he teaches marketing and sustainability-related courses.

Chapter 1
Introduction

Packaging is a multifaceted element that plays a central role in marketing strategy. Beyond serving its traditional function as a product container, packaging has evolved into a powerful marketing tool that influences consumer perception, evaluation, and choice. It shapes in-store purchase decisions, often serving as the first point of contact between consumers and products (Festila & Chrysochou, 2018; Herédia-Colaço, 2023; Liao et al., 2015; Park & Ma, 2019). Consumers often rely on packaging features to evaluate products, even without seeing the actual item (Holmes & Paswan, 2012; Söderlund et al., 2017). It can convey product attributes and brand values, stimulate desire, and affect judgments about quality, sustainability, and attractiveness (Briand Decré & Cloonan, 2019; Chen, 2021; Coelho do Vale & Verga Matos, 2015; Park & Ma, 2019; Söderlund et al., 2017). Some firms could invest more in packaging design than in advertising, underlining its strategic importance (Söderlund et al., 2017).

At the same time, packaging has increasingly been scrutinized because of its impact on the environment. Indeed, sustainability has become a critical concern in packaging design, reflecting growing consumer expectations and regulatory pressures. Packaging waste represents a major environmental issue, especially for fast-moving consumer goods (FMCGs). Consumers increasingly expect packaging to reflect environmental responsibility, and marketers must now integrate ecological considerations into design choices (e.g., Akturan et al., 2025; Branca et al., 2024b; Herbes et al., 2020). In this context, sustainability considerations add a further layer of complexity to packaging evaluation, requiring marketers to balance aesthetic appeal, usability, and ecological responsibility.

Thus, packaging is an integral element directly associated with a product, one that many products cannot exist or be commercialized without, and plays an important role in influencing consumers' perceptions and purchasing behaviors. However, in today's increasingly interconnected and digital world, product managers are confronted with a new challenge: the emergence of Virtual Reality (VR). VR is steadily garnering attention from both academics and practitioners, also due to its growing societal

G. Branca, *Virtual Reality, Real Intentions*, International Series in Advanced Management Studies, https://doi.org/10.1007/978-3-032-10142-6_1

relevance (Branca et al., 2024a). VR enables users to disconnect from the external world and immerse themselves in a digital realm, where they can interact with digital objects in real time (Hilken et al., 2022). VR is also a key technology contributing to the development of the metaverse, a topic of debate in the recent marketing scientific community (Dwivedi et al., 2022). VR has reached a level of maturity, and it is more accessible for consumers than before (Corallo et al., 2020), with significant anticipated impacts in retail and shopping (Martínez-Navarro et al., 2019; Xi & Hamari, 2021). VR can replicate real-life scenarios but also provide entirely new shopping experiences that were previously inconceivable. Consumers will be able to navigate in VR and purchase either virtual or real products.

Given packaging's relevance, particularly in FMCG categories, its role in VR environments warrants careful investigation. Since packaging is tightly linked to product choice and brand evaluation, understanding how it is perceived in VR compared to Physical Reality (PR) is essential. Existing literature has paid limited attention to this issue. Most of the existing studies on packaging have focused on in-store or physical settings, with limited attention to online, augmented, or virtual marketplaces (Akturan et al., 2025). Yet, as consumer behavior increasingly shifts toward immersive digital environments, packaging research must evolve to explore the dynamics of these contexts. Importantly, even if product interaction occurs in VR, the eventual consumption of the physical good could take place in the real world, reinforcing the need to understand the implications of virtual evaluations on physical-world behaviors (Rodrigues & Loureiro, 2022). This research also emphasizes sustainability as a unifying theme that intersects both packaging design and VR technology. Beyond being a relevant trend in consumer expectations and regulatory agendas, sustainability introduces significant challenges to packaging development, such as material innovation, waste reduction, and life cycle transparency. VR can play a crucial role in addressing these challenges by enabling cost-effective, low-waste testing of eco-friendly packaging prototypes, and facilitating research into consumer perceptions of sustainable cues in realistic contexts. By integrating these dimensions, this monograph aims to advance not only the understanding of consumer behavior in immersive environments but also the role of VR in supporting environmentally responsible innovation and the sustainability perceptions of packaging alternatives.

These underexplored areas raise several critical questions.

- *How do consumers evaluate packaged products in VR compared to PR?*
- *Are there differences in consumer responses between these two conditions?*

Our understanding of consumer behavior in VR within this context is still limited, and marketing literature has only recently developed (Branca et al., 2023; Wedel et al., 2020). Still, it remains unclear whether VR can produce responses similar enough to PR to serve as a valid environment for packaging evaluation and research. Packaging is gaining recognition as a three-dimensional marketing communication medium (Coelho do Vale & Verga Matos, 2015) and previous literature has demonstrated that physically touching a product increases product evaluation compared to merely viewing a picture in a remote environment. Additionally, the weight of an object influences perceived value (Briand Decré & Cloonan, 2019). The sensory cues present in PR interactions are still absent in VR, while touch plays a crucial role in product evaluation, even in situations where physical touch is not possible, such as online shopping (Briand Decré & Cloonan, 2019). However, even if consumers achieve the same product evaluation both in VR and PR, it should be clarified if they generate the same attitudinal and behavioral responses.

This volume addresses these gaps by comparing how consumers evaluate packaged products in VR versus PR. Building on a preliminary qualitative study and a mixed-design experimental approach, it examines responses to different packaging attributes, namely structural, haptic, and visual cues, in both environments. The results demonstrate that while some minor differences emerge, consumer evaluations are broadly consistent across VR and PR, reinforcing the potential of VR as a research environment for packaging studies.

This volume is organized as follows.

Chapter 2 explores the use of VR in marketing literature and product research via a comprehensive review, building on Branca et al. (2024a). The aim is to get an overview of the research progress on the topic, frame the gap in the literature to fill in with the present research, and obtain useful insights and directions for the development of the overall study. The chapter also deepens the methodological aspects related to research conducted in VR, shows how VR has been employed—standing alone or in combination with other technologies—in consumer behavior studies and highlights differences between VR and other experimental conditions.

Chapter 3 addresses packaging literature, especially under the sustainability light, building on Branca et al. (2024b), synthesizing previous contributions on eco-friendly packaging cues in the consumer behavior domain. The review classifies the research by identifying four main themes: consumers' knowledge and understanding of sustainable packaging; studies that investigate green packaging following a holistic approach; studies employing an analytical approach to identifying potentially important package cues; and investigations of consumers' attitudes and behaviors toward eco-friendly packaging. This review leads to a clear overview of the literature progress on the topic but also helps better structure this research: through the results, it derived a better understanding of how to develop the packaging manipulations used as a basis for the experimental study. It seemed appropriate to consider packaging cues of a different type since consumers' responses could vary according to the nature of the presented stimuli.

Chapter 4 outlines research questions, hypotheses, and the methodological approach. It builds on Branca et al. (2023) and integrates insights from the literature reviews on VR and packaging to develop a set of testable hypotheses focused on consumers' evaluations of packaging across virtual and physical environments. The chapter also describes the experimental design, detailing the structure of the mixed-method approach and the manipulations employed in this research.

Chapter 5 presents the preliminary study (two focus groups) and procedural setup of the empirical analysis, presented in detail in the following chapters.

Chapters 6, 7, and 8 report the results of the three experimental studies. Each chapter focuses on a specific packaging cue and details the effects on consumer perceptions, attitudes, and behavioral intentions. The analyses examine differences and consistencies between the VR and PR conditions across multiple dependent variables, namely perceived sustainability, willingness to pay a premium price, purchase intention, attitude toward packaging, perceived quality, and attractiveness. The chapters also include discussions that interpret the results considering the proposed hypotheses and theoretical background.

Chapter 9 provides an integrative discussion of the findings across all studies. It highlights the theoretical and managerial implications of using VR for packaging evaluation and test, and outlines the methodological contributions of the research. The chapter concludes by addressing the limitations of the current research and proposing directions for future studies, with a focus on advancing the role of immersive technologies in consumer research and experimental marketing. Finally, Chap. 10 highlights the main conclusions of the volume.

This manuscript presents the complete outcomes of the research project conducted over three years by the author as part of the Ph.D. Programme "Person, Market, Institution" at the Department of Law, Economics, Management and Quantitative Methods (DEMM), University of Sannio, Italy. The Ph.D. thesis titled "*Consumers' evaluations of product packaging in Virtual Reality and Real Life: a comparative experimental analysis*" was developed under the supervision of Professor Riccardo Resciniti, University of Sannio. Parts of the study have already been disseminated through presentations at international conferences and have led to the publication of three scientific articles: Branca et al. (2023, 2024a, 2024b).

References

Akturan, U., Kuter, D., & Gökkut, B. S. (2025). Mirror, mirror on the wall, who is the most convincing of them all? A systematic literature review on packaging. *Journal of Business Research, 193*, Article 115355. https://doi.org/10.1016/j.jbusres.2025.115355

Branca, G., Marino, V., & Resciniti, R. (2024a). How do consumers evaluate products in virtual reality? A literature review for a research agenda. *Spanish Journal of Marketing—ESIC, 28*(3), 356–380. https://doi.org/10.1108/SJME-07-2022-0153

Branca, G., Resciniti, R., & Babin, B. J. (2024b). Sustainable packaging design and the consumer perspective: A systematic literature review. *Italian Journal of Marketing*, 77–111. https://doi.org/10.1007/s43039-023-00084-1

Branca, G., Resciniti, R., & Loureiro, S. M. C. (2023). Virtual is so real! Consumers' evaluation of product packaging in virtual reality. *Psychology & Marketing, 40*, 596–609. https://doi.org/10.1002/mar.21743

Briand Decré, G., & Cloonan, C. (2019). A touch of gloss: Haptic perception of packaging and consumers' reactions. *Journal of Product & Brand Management, 28*(1), 117–132. https://doi.org/10.1108/JPBM-05-2017-1472

Chen, Y. S. A. (2021). Does outward appearance appeal to the inward mind? The impact of packaging finishes on brand impressions and the subsequent behavior of consumer. *Journal of Product & Brand Management, 30*(5), 768–778. https://doi.org/10.1108/JPBM-07-2019-2466

Coelho do Vale, R., & Verga Matos, P. (2015). The impact of copycat packaging strategies on the adoption of private labels. *Journal of Product & Brand Management, 24*(6), 646–659. https://doi.org/10.1108/JPBM-03-2015-0846

Corallo, A., Lazoi, M., Papadia, G., & Pascarelli, C. (2020). Action research on Virtual-Reality-Assisted product and process design. *IEEE Transactions on Engineering Management*, 1–18. https://doi.org/10.1109/TEM.2020.3038461

Dwivedi, Y. K., Hughes, L., Baabdullah, A. M., Ribeiro-Navarrete, S., Giannakis, M., Al-Debei, M. M., Dennehy, D., Metri, B., Buhalis, D., Cheung, C. M., Conboy, K., Doyle, R., Dubey, R., Dutot, V., Felix, R., Goyal, D. P., Gustafsson, A., Hinsch, C., Jebabli, I., …, Wamba, S. F. (2022). Metaverse beyond the hype: Multidisciplinary perspectives on emerging challenges, opportunities, and agenda for research, practice and policy. *International Journal of Information Management, 66*, 102542. https://doi.org/10.1016/j.ijinfomgt.2022.102542

Festila, A., & Chrysochou, P. (2018). Implicit communication of food product healthfulness through package design: A content analysis. *Journal of Consumer Behavior, 17*, 461–476. https://doi.org/10.1002/cb.1732

Herbes, C., Beuthner, C., & Ramme, I. (2020). How green is your packaging—A comparative international study of cues consumers use to recognize environmentally friendly packaging. *International Journal of Consumer Studies, 44*(3), 258–271. https://doi.org/10.1111/ijcs.12560

Herédia-Colaço, V. (2023). Pro-environmental messages have more effect when they come from less familiar brands. *Journal of Product & Brand Management, 32*(3), 436–453. https://doi.org/10.1108/JPBM-12-2021-3782

Hilken, T., Chylinski, M., Keeling, D. I., Heller, J., Ruyter, K., & Mahr, D. (2022). How to strategically choose or combine augmented and virtual reality for improved online experiential retailing. *Psychology & Marketing, 39*, 495–507. https://doi.org/10.1002/mar.21600

Holmes, G. R., & Paswan, A. (2012). Consumer reaction to new package design. *Journal of Product & Brand Management, 21*(2), 109–116. https://doi.org/10.1108/10610421211215553

Liao, L. L., Corsi, A. M., Chrysochou, P., & Larry Lockshin, L. (2015). Emotional responses towards food packaging: A joint application of self-report and physiological measures of emotion. *Food Quality and Preference, 42*, 48–55. https://doi.org/10.1016/j.foodqual.2015.01.009

Martínez-Navarro, J., Bigné, E., Guixeres, J., Alcañiz, M., & Torrecilla, C. (2019). The influence of virtual reality in e-commerce. *Journal of Business Research, 100*, 475–482. https://doi.org/10.1016/j.jbusres.2018.10.054

Park, J., & Ma, Y. J. (2019). Number-location bias: Do consumers correctly process the number on the product package? *Journal of Product & Brand Management, 28*(1), 80–94. https://doi.org/10.1108/JPBM-12-2017-1711

Rodrigues, M. B., & Loureiro, S. M. C. (2022). Virtual reality in the motion picture industry: The relationship among movie coolness, sympathy, empathy, and word-of-mouth. *Journal of Promotion Management, 28*(2), 144–159. https://doi.org/10.1080/10496491.2021.1987964

Söderlund, M., Colliander, J., Karsberg, J., Liljedal, K. T., Modig, E., Rosengren, S., Sagfossen, S., Szugalski, S., & Åkestam, N. (2017). The allure of the bottle as a package: An assessment of perceived effort in a packaging context. *Journal of Product & Brand Management, 26*(1), 91–100. https://doi.org/10.1108/JPBM-12-2015-1065

Wedel, M., Bigné, E., & Zhang, J. (2020). Virtual and augmented reality: Advancing research in consumer marketing. *International Journal of Research in Marketing, 37*(3), 443–465. https://doi.org/10.1016/j.ijresmar.2020.04.004

Xi, N., & Hamari, J. (2021). Shopping in virtual reality: A literature review and future agenda. *Journal of Business Research, 134*, 37–58. https://doi.org/10.1016/j.jbusres.2021.04.075

Chapter 2
Virtual Reality in Marketing: Consumer and Product Research

2.1 Virtual Reality

The relevance of Virtual Reality (VR) in the business context and the academic debate is growing rapidly. VR regarded as a synthetic environment (Loureiro et al., 2019) already finds application in several contexts, such as tourism, product development, advertising, entertainment, healthcare, education, marketing, architecture, training, and retail (Fares et al., 2024). It is considered a technological megatrend progressing the digitization of all areas of human life (Xi & Hamari, 2021).

The consumer VR market was projected to increase from 16 billion U.S. dollars in 2024 to more than 18 billion U.S. dollars by the end of 2025 (Statista, 2024). According to PWC (2019), the major business use cases for VR will be product and service development, healthcare, development and training, process improvements, retail, and consumers. As a key enabler of the metaverse, VR is emerging as a major technological trend with significant implications for consumer behavior (Dwivedi et al., 2022; Xi & Hamari, 2021). The Extended Reality (XR) technologies, which include VR and Augmented Reality (AR), are central to the transformation of e-commerce into x-commerce, capable of replicating the multisensory engagement of physical stores and enriching consumer experiences (Chen et al., 2024).

Indeed, VR is gaining prominence as a valuable marketing platform. Its applications are now widespread across various sectors, with retail and shopping emerging as particularly promising areas, since VR can provide consumers with a new shopping experience (e.g., Bigné et al., 2024; Han et al., 2020; Martínez-Navarro et al., 2019; Rodrigues & Loureiro, 2022; van Berlo et al., 2021). Companies such as Meta, Amazon, Alibaba, Walmart, IKEA, Macy's, and eBay, have long invested in this technology (Chen et al., 2024; Kinzinger et al., 2025; Xi & Hamari, 2021), and several brands are leveraging immersive digital technologies, as VR, to deliver highly personalized and customizable experiences, to drive more favorable consumer evaluations (Alexander et al., 2025). VR applications are entering a phase of maturity, which features high-performance and immersive devices, such as Head Mounted Displays

G. Branca, *Virtual Reality, Real Intentions*, International Series in Advanced Management Studies, https://doi.org/10.1007/978-3-032-10142-6_2

(HMDs), more affordable and accessible to consumers (Flavián et al., 2019a), integrated with sophisticated motion-tracking systems that can offer immersive experiences (Fares et al., 2024), pushing companies to resort to virtual environments such as experiential marketing platforms (Corallo et al., 2020; van Berlo et al., 2021). The mainstream adoption of VR allows realistic and engaging experiences for consumers (Deloitte, 2023). Currently, some of the most relevant HMD suppliers include Meta, Microsoft, Sony, and Pico (Fares et al., 2024; Statista, 2024). Indeed, retailers are rethinking their strategies to stay competitive in an increasingly virtual marketplace, with VR headsets expected to become the primary medium for accessing virtual environments due to the greater intuitiveness of 3D interactions compared to 2D experiences (Marx et al., 2025).

Research on applied VR took the first steps back in the 1990s (Loureiro et al., 2019), but marketing literature on VR is only recently advancing (Wedel et al., 2020), differently from other academic fields, such as engineering, psychology, and computer science. Knowledge about VR in marketing should be deepened, as there seems to be little consensus among researchers on how consumers respond to this technology, and insight into marketing-based VR applications and peculiarities in consumers' attitudes and behavior in VR are needed (Cowan et al., 2021; Hollebeek et al., 2020; Wedel et al., 2020). In this line, researchers need to expand existing consumer behavior concepts and theories considering VR practices and applications (Wedel et al., 2020). Xi and Hamari (2021) highlight how findings of differences between VR and other shopping environments showed mixed results, and literature calls for more research that compares behavior in VR versus PR (Pfeiffer et al., 2020; Siegrist et al., 2019). Indeed, greater attention is needed on how consumers evaluate products in VR, particularly within retail settings (Kim et al., 2021), and how they behave in virtual environments (e.g., Bigné et al., 2024; Schnack et al., 2020). Unlike applications in tourism or hospitality, VR in a shopping environment requires consumers to actively assess and judge virtual products, not just experience the environment itself. As multisensory experiences in VR may be context-specific (Mishra et al., 2021), evaluations can vary significantly, for instance, between a virtual tourism destination and a gaming scenario. The differences between tangible and intangible contexts, like between retail and hospitality, can lead to different results (Orús et al., 2021).

In addition, VR also represents a useful tool for marketers because it allows them to obtain benefits over traditional research methods, leading to researchers' greater control and creating new ways of studying consumption and marketing. VR can lead to the development of models that allow efficient and rigorous research in the consumer behavior domain (Siegrist et al., 2019) since it is characterized by high ecological validity (Meißner et al., 2020). This technology broadens the research boundaries, enabling the study of alternative realities and new product ideas, facilitating experiments that could not be easily conducted traditionally, due to the costs, operational difficulties, or the perishable nature of the products (Lombart et al., 2019; Siegrist et al., 2019). Studies in VR may not suffer from limits on space and time in conducting research, and settings can be promptly modified or reproduced, according to researchers' needs. In this line, Hoyer et al. (2020) underline how this technology can be relevant in the pre-transaction phase and in stimulating curiosity and desire to try new products in consumers. Schnack et al. (2020) highlight how several effects of marketing interventions, such as food packaging design or advertising, can be tested via VR. Moreover, Hube et al. (2020) underline the role of VR in early design phases, especially for rapid prototyping and product design evaluation. This process would thus prove to be shorter and less expensive (Bu et al., 2021). Indeed, simulating real products and packaging can influence the shopping experience and enhance brands by affecting product attributes and information (Loureiro et al., 2019). van Berlo et al. (2021) argue that VR does not need to perfectly mimic PR to allow for virtual product appraisal. According to Huang et al. (2021), VR represents a useful approach in packaging prototyping, elicits a searching process similar to PR, and delivers realistic cues for food and beverage products.

Building on these considerations, the following sections will deepen the understanding of VR in marketing and product research by reviewing relevant and recent literature. First, Sect. 2.2 provides an overview of definitions and taxonomies used to frame VR within the marketing literature. Then, Sect. 2.3 explores how products are evaluated, and how consumers respond within VR environments. Section 2.4 focuses on VR as a research environment, highlighting its methodological contributions and comparing VR to other experimental conditions. Finally, the last sections synthesize the main findings of this chapter. This chapter offers a comprehensive foundation for positioning VR not only as a technological tool, but also as an effective and rigorous environment for studying consumer behavior and delivering new experiences to shoppers.

2.2 Virtual Reality in the Marketing Literature

VR refers to "*computer generated simulation experience delivered through a technological application*", as claimed by Dietrich et al. (2019, p. 806), according to Biocca and Levy (1995) and Krueger (1991). As highlighted by Loureiro et al. (2019, p. 514), according to Milgram et al. (1994), VR may be defined as the environment "*in which the participant-observer is totally immersed in a completely synthetic world, which may or may not mimic the properties of a real-world environment*". Cowan and Ketron (2019a, p. 483), according to Berg and Vance (2017) and Guttentag (2010), claim that VR is "*the application of three-dimensional computer technology to generate a virtual environment within which users navigate and interact*". Furthermore, as pointed out by Wedel et al. (2020, p. 443), according to LaValle (2017) and Sherman and Craig (2002), VR is a "*computer-generated simulation of a situation that incorporates the user, who perceives it via one or more of the senses (currently mostly vision, hearing and touch), and interacts with it in a manner that appears to be real*". As highlighted by Lee et al. (2020, p. 2), according to Barnes (2016), VR "*provide potential consumers with the most realistic experience of a product, service or place yet without necessary physical co-location*".

In VR, users are immersed in interactive 3D environments that enable navigation and elicit sensory stimulation (Flavián et al., 2021). VR creates a strong sense of presence in a digitally fabricated environment, unlike other media (Kang et al., 2020). Pala et al. (2021) claim that VR combines kinetic, visual, and audio components in a virtual environment and generates immersion and engagement. VR allows isolating individuals from the outside world, immersing them in a complete and innovative synthetic environment (Hoyer et al., 2020; Loureiro et al., 2019). Users can interact in real time and move physically within the virtual environment (Cowan & Ketron, 2019b; Hoyer et al., 2020), being isolated from the real world. VR possesses distinctive features that differentiate it from the other XR technologies (Flavián et al., 2019b).

A foundational model in this domain is the "*Reality–Virtuality Continuum*" developed by Milgram and Kishino (1994), which classifies experiences along a spectrum from fully real to fully virtual. Flavián et al. (2019b) expanded this framework by introducing an additional category, Pure Mixed Reality (PMR), to better capture the integration of physical and digital elements. According to the authors, at one end of the continuum lies the real environment, where users interact solely with physical elements. The other end is the virtual environment, including both VR and Virtual Worlds, which are digital spaces, like Second Life, where avatars can interact in real time. However, the term VR has often been misapplied to other technologies such as Virtual Worlds, the internet, or various digital platforms (Xi & Hamari, 2021). Between these extremes are hybrid forms: (a) AR, which overlays digital content onto the physical world, enhancing real-world experiences (Heller et al., 2021); (b) Augmented Virtuality (AV), which overlays real-world elements onto a virtual setting; and (c) PMR, which blends both realms, allowing users to interact simultaneously with real and virtual elements in an integrated way. Each reality type is distinct, with its own characteristics and interaction modes.

To further clarify this landscape, Flavián et al. (2019b) proposed the EPI Cube, a three-dimensional framework that maps reality technologies based on technological embodiment, perceptual presence, and behavioral interactivity. Among its categories, Vertices 7 and 8 are especially relevant to this research, corresponding to 360° videos viewed via HMDs and fully immersive VR HMDs, respectively.

Different types of VR can be identified in marketing literature. Cowan and Ketron (2019b) propose a framework based on user immersion and user experience. The applications that fall under the name of Automated Virtual Environment ensure the highest level of user experience and realism: users can look around, move, and interact with features and objects, in a realistic and completely immersive environment. This category includes applications with HMDs, a solution that leads to the highest degree of immersion, and Cave Automatic Virtual Environment (CAVE). Other categories, i.e., Simulations, Virtual Worlds and Games, present lower levels of user experience, realism, or both. Virtual Worlds and Games are not considered in this research since the user experience is oriented toward a fantasy world. Simulations, instead, may be marginally considered for the purpose of identifying potentially interesting studies on product trials.

A categorization of VR archetypes is provided by Hollebeek et al. (2020), moving from academic, consultancy, and practitioner sources. The authors propose a framework based on autonomous/programmatic VR platforms and VR centric/non-VR centric VR, developing a matrix that includes 4 archetypes.

To conclude, although VR has been studied and deepened in other areas of marketing, such as hospitality and tourism, there seem to be few reviews that have studied consumer behavior in VR, focusing on product evaluation and testing, and differences between VR and other experimental conditions in product tests. This gap is addressed by Branca et al. (2024) who systematically review how consumers evaluate products in VR. In addition, Xi and Hamari (2021) propose a literature review on shopping in VR. Among others, some findings show mixed results about the differences between VR and other shopping environments. Authors call for progression in VR literature in methodological rigor and theoretical application. In this line, VR should be studied not only as a purchasing environment but also as a new environment and methodology for product research. As mentioned, VR opens new scenarios and opportunities to marketing scholars and gives several benefits over traditional research methods. VR may create new ways of conducting research and, therefore, deserves a focused analysis.

2.3 Products and Consumers in Virtual Reality

Understanding how consumers assess products in VR is critical for advancing both theory and practice in marketing. While traditional digital commerce environments offer limited sensory and spatial cues, VR introduces a highly immersive and interactive context that can more closely mimic (and enrich) the physical shopping experience, overcoming many of the limitations of traditional e-commerce (Luna-Nevarez & McGovern, 2021). By offering immersive, always-accessible experiences, VR enhances consumer engagement and supports multisensory interaction, simplifying decision-making (Mishra et al., 2021). This section focuses on two core dimensions emerging from the literature: the evaluation of products in VR and the consumer responses in VR. Together, they provide insights into how VR-specific features shape consumer judgments, preferences, and behaviors.

2.3.1 Products in Virtual Reality

VR can provide realistic cues for food and beverage products, facilitating intuitive and natural search behaviors (Bigné et al., 2016; Huang et al., 2021), further supporting its potential as a retail interface. However, product evaluation in VR does not require a literal replication of brick-and-mortar settings to be effective (van Berlo et al., 2021). Its immersive nature can simulate conditions close to physical retail, particularly when interactivity is high (Peukert et al., 2019). In these environments, the stimuli quality and resolution are relevant in product diagnosticity, and vivid stimuli enhance hedonic experiences via telepresence. Moreover, Kang et al. (2020) noted that in 3D virtual contexts, users often overlook graphic detail, possibly because other spatial and sensory cues dominate attention. Interactivity, such as product manipulation, and visual-spatial cues, such as visualizing a full-size product in 3D, influence both perceived informativeness and the overall enjoyment of the experience. Allowing consumers to test product functions in an immersive VR environment can significantly enhance their shopping experience, with hedonic factors such as enjoyment playing a crucial role in shaping their perceptions of immersive webshops (Kinzinger et al., 2025).

The role of product type is also relevant but presents mixed results. Utilitarian items tend to yield stronger purchase intentions in VR, perhaps because the environment adds stimulation to otherwise ordinary choices (Mishra et al., 2021). However, according to Lee et al. (2025), VR is more effective for hedonic products, since it can boost hedonic benefits but may reduce utilitarian ones, particularly for consumers with a utilitarian orientation. Literature also found that consumers are more responsive to products perceived as extensions of the body, like tools, compared to presentations of the body, such as clothing (Alzayat & Lee, 2021). As discussed by Bigné et al. (2024), semidurable goods (i.e., sneakers) required more extensive information gathering and processing than FMCGs (i.e., snacks), suggesting differences in decision-making processes, depending on product category, and indicating that shopping behavior in VR closely mirrors that in real-life contexts. Moreover, high-involvement products (e.g., expensive or high-risk items) favor the effectiveness of VR, even for knowledgeable consumers, since it better supports decision-making by facilitating mental imagery and reducing uncertainty (Zhang et al., 2024). Finally, Zhang et al. (2025) present product interactivity, graspability, and haptic feedback as boundary conditions, offering a decision framework for retailers to align VR investments with product features and shopping contexts.

VR benefits seem not to be uniform across all evaluation dimensions. For example, while VR increases realism and engagement (Kim et al., 2021), it does not consistently improve choice satisfaction, especially when users cannot judge the product accurately (Meißner et al., 2020). Still, it can reduce sensory mismatches—such as the color–flavor incongruence—which improves product evaluation, although the same mitigation is not observed in brand-related judgments (Huang & Wan, 2019). Even outside traditional shopping contexts, product aesthetics in VR environments can improve brand attitudes, though this does not always translate into increased purchase intent (van Berlo et al., 2021). Moreover, as highlighted by Uysal et al. (2025), VR product presentations do not intrinsically improve consumer outcomes. It can benefit retailers when they showcase hedonic products, use interactive and realistic environments to trigger product imagination, show products in a congruent usage context, and allow virtual product assembly.

A key element of VR lies in the possibility of simulating haptic feedback. While actual touch is absent, virtual haptic simulations can approximate tactile interaction effectively (Alzayat & Lee, 2021). Sensory inputs remain essential to product evaluation, with manipulability and auditory cues affecting brand perceptions (Cowan et al.,

2021; Ringler et al., 2021). Nevertheless, the user's need for touch could moderate this relationship: those with higher tactile sensitivity tend to derive less hedonic value from VR shopping (Alzayat & Lee, 2021). According to Luangrath et al. (2022), the vicarious haptic effect is particularly strong among individuals who feel deeply immersed in a VR experience. This heightened immersion enhances the sense of body ownership, which in turn fosters psychological ownership of the product and leads to more favorable product evaluations.

However, despite these elements, the absence of certain sensory inputs, such as smell or temperature, may limit behavioral responses, particularly in individuals whose personalities are more reliant on such cues (Schnack et al., 2021a).

2.3.2 *Consumers in Virtual Reality*

Consumer behavior in VR environments is often comparable to real-world shopping, yet it also reflects unique dynamics. VR stores can increase consumer attention and word-of-mouth (WOM) recommendations, encourage deeper product inspection, and trigger impulse purchases (Mishra et al., 2021; Schnack et al., 2021a). In such environments, consumers can exhibit lower price sensitivity (Meißner et al., 2020; Peukert et al., 2019). Lee et al. (2025) highlighted that environment-replicating VR enhances engagement throughout the consumer journey, leading to increased consumption and improved retention.

Brand evaluation and purchase intention in VR are shaped by multiple factors, including product familiarity, presence induced and haptic input (Cowan et al., 2021). However, a high sense of presence does not necessarily improve memory-based outcomes such as brand recall (van Berlo et al., 2021).

VR becomes particularly influential in playful, high-immersion settings, where aesthetic appeal affects consumer judgments (Kang et al., 2020). Body ownership and control enhance both perceived usefulness and enjoyment (Han et al., 2020). These perceptions serve as important predictors of store visit and purchase intentions. In this line, consumers' sense of pleasure, stimulated by the escapist nature of the VR experience, enhances the vividness and presence of the virtual store. This leads to stronger behavioral intentions, such as the desire to revisit the store or recommend it to others (Loureiro et al., 2021). Moreover, Marx et al. (2025) suggested integrating audio priming into VR applications to familiarize consumers with the technology behind the experience. This simple and cost-effective approach can improve processing fluency, foster familiarity, and enhance spatial presence, ultimately leading to a more positive consumer response.

Emotional responses elicited in VR enhance the sense of presence and positively influence purchase intentions. The affective evaluation of VR supports brand recall, which further contributes to consumers' intention to buy (Martínez-Navarro et al., 2019). Interactions with brands in VR can generate emotional reactions along both arousal and valence dimensions (van Berlo et al., 2021). These emotional responses raise the perceived hedonic value of the brand, ultimately driving consumer commercial behavior.

Literature shows that shopping behavior in VR is often consistent with offline patterns, especially during multi-category trips (Huang et al., 2021; Schnack et al., 2020), when the VR environment replicates a well-structured store layout (Peukert et al., 2019). VR appears effective for consumers in a browsing mindset, where exploration is central to the experience (Park & Kim, 2021). Finally, while VR offers superior product visualization compared to standard e-commerce, its level of interactivity may still fall short of that found in physical retail settings (Kim et al., 2021).

2.4 Virtual Reality as a Research Environment

VR has an appealing potential as a research tool in marketing and consumer behavior studies. VR offers a unique setting for analyzing consumer behavior, search, interactions, and purchases between competing brands (Bigné et al., 2024). Beyond replicating real-world shopping environments, VR enables controlled, immersive, and interactive experiences that can generate ecologically valid consumer insights while overcoming many logistical and methodological limitations of traditional research methods.

The following sections explore VR's role as an experimental condition and in comparison with other experimental environments, highlighting its advantages and challenges in marketing research.

2.4.1 Virtual Reality as an Experimental Condition

VR is increasingly recognized as a convincing experimental tool for product testing and consumer research. Its ability to create immersive, interactive, and controllable environments allows researchers to observe realistic consumer behavior under high ecological validity (Harz et al., 2021; Meißner et al., 2019). VR provides an immersive and lifelike shopping experience, enabling consumers to examine products in high detail (Zhang et al., 2025). Moreover, VR environments, such as VR supermarkets, enable researchers to observe brand choices and behavioral processes in conditions that minimize the limitations associated with field studies, increasing choice realism and deeper evaluation processes (Bernritter et al., 2021; Esmark Jones et al., 2018; Ketelaar et al., 2017; Pfeiffer et al., 2020). Thus, it provides a suitable solution for generalizing findings to real-world retail contexts, offering strong external validity, minimizing external influences, and generating richer behavioral data (Dwivedi et al., 2022; Lombart et al., 2019; Meißner et al., 2019; Siegrist et al., 2019). Indeed, compared to traditional methods, VR allows researchers to measure variables such as decision paths, gaze patterns, and handling times, i.e., metrics often inaccessible in traditional settings and difficult to capture in physical or online studies (Esmark Jones et al., 2018; Ketelaar et al., 2017, 2018).

Empirical studies confirm that consumer behavior in VR settings is consistent and realistic (Harz et al., 2021), and the immersive experience can even help participants form a more complete understanding of products (Naderi et al., 2020).

VR also simplifies experimental manipulation, making it particularly effective for prototyping, product evaluation, and packaging design testing, by enabling rapid adjustments and repeatability (Hoyer et al., 2020; Huang et al., 2021; Hube et al., 2020; Schnack et al., 2020). Indeed, it addresses many limitations of traditional research by enabling real-time adjustments to product features and reducing challenges related to cost, complexity, time, availability, and perishability. As Harz et al. (2021) note, VR-based lab studies offer predictive advantages over online or conventional testing and are highly applicable in early product development phases, allowing firms to work with virtual prototypes. In the food and beverage domain, VR proves especially beneficial. As an example, Lombart et al. (2019) used a virtual grocery store to test consumer responses to fresh produce with varying degrees of deformity. The study showed consistent purchasing behavior across conditions and highlighted VR's usefulness for testing perishable items, eliminating issues related to spoilage, waste, and logistical constraints.

While VR offers substantial benefits, researchers must consider how data collection methods may influence results. Schnack et al. (2021a) emphasized that differences between VR and physical settings may stem from reliance on subjective versus objective instruments. Traditional research often depends on self-reported data, which can introduce bias. To address this, several studies have combined VR with biometric or cognitive tracking technologies. For example, Bernritter et al. (2021) used eye-tracking to monitor visual attention in real time during VR experiments, while Bigné et al. (2016) integrated a CAVE system with eye-tracking. Harz et al. (2021) further applied motion-tracking sensors to enhance interaction analysis. Meißner et al. (2019) provided an analysis of integrating eye-tracking across VR, desktop, and physical environments. Huang et al. (2021) combined VR with resting-state fMRI to explore neural responses during product search, while Schnack et al. (2021b) employed EEG to examine consumer reactions in VR.

2.4.2 Comparison of Virtual Reality with Other Experimental Conditions

VR presents notable advantages. However, it is essential to compare its features and effectiveness with other experimental environments and conditions, to fully understand its potential and limitations in consumer research.

Pfeiffer et al. (2020) highlighted strong similarities between physical and virtual supermarkets, emphasizing the importance of comparative studies that assess consumer responses across these environments. In some respects, VR stores may even outperform physical stores, eliciting more favorable consumer reactions. Martínez-Navarro et al. (2019) examined different VR formats and devices, finding that HMDs deliver higher levels of presence compared to powerwalls, although they also tend to produce more physical discomfort than PCs. Notably, this discomfort did not negatively impact the sense of presence or brand recall, making it the only relative drawback of VR versus physical environments. Across various VR formats, including 3D and 360°, cognitive and affective responses remained consistent, with format primarily affecting purchase intention. Brand recall was significantly higher in all VR conditions compared to physical stores, and VR also led to increased purchase intentions.

Immersive VR also appears to foster more exploratory consumer behavior. Meißner et al. (2020) found that consumers in immersive VR environments exhibit stronger variety-seeking tendencies, although this does not necessarily translate into greater satisfaction with their choices when compared to non-immersive VR. Harz et al. (2021) compared laboratory VR, online VR, and physical product testing, concluding that lab-based VR yielded more consistent consumer behavior. This was attributed to the enhanced vividness and presence experienced in immersive settings. According to Zhang et al. (2025), immersive VR increases purchase intention by enhancing product diagnosticity, compared to non-immersive VR, but this advantage depends on context. Immersive VR is most beneficial when product interactivity is low, compensating for limited consumer-product engagement. Under high interactivity, immersive VR retains its advantage mainly for graspable products or when haptic information is provided for non-graspable products. Without haptic cues, non-immersive VR performs equally well and is more cost-effective.

Cowan et al. (2021) investigated the effects of 360° VR in online versus in-store contexts and found that online use of 360° VR was more effective in shaping brand responses. However, this advantage diminished among consumers with high category knowledge, who reported lower brand attitudes and purchase intentions in 360° VR environments. When haptic cues were introduced, these negative effects were mitigated. In this line, Zhang et al. (2024) found that VR retail effectiveness does not always outperform static images, since its advantage diminishes for consumers with high product knowledge.

Kim et al. (2022) reported that VR environments foster higher immersion than websites, enhancing the flow experience and leading to a greater intention to visit the physical store. While VR was found to improve the hedonic value of shopping compared to standard websites, it had less effect on utilitarian value. This influence was mediated by telepresence, i.e., the sensation of being present in a virtual space (Alzayat & Lee, 2021). Pizzi et al. (2020) showed that VR environments generate a stronger sense of presence than physical stores, regardless of consumers' technological confidence. This enhanced presence positively shaped the shopping experience, increasing perceived value, purchase intentions, and WOM. Conversely, Kang et al. (2020) found that 3D VR stores led to lower purchase intentions than 3D web environments, possibly due to lower perceived informativeness in the VR context.

Comparative studies of the diverse immersive technologies further clarify their respective strengths. Mishra et al. (2021) showed that VR elicits higher purchase intentions than mobile apps for utilitarian products, while AR provides better experience for hedonic products. Park and Kim (2021) found that when consumers are in a browsing mindset, VR outperforms AR and static images in boosting clothing purchase intention. In contrast, for searching tasks, both VR and AR exceed static images. According to Hilken et al. (2022), AR is generally more effective in increasing purchase intentions, whereas VR is stronger in enhancing brand attitudes. The combination of AR and VR can improve both outcomes, but only when VR follows AR. This sequence aligns with the logic of the online-to-offline shopping journey, where AR facilitates product selection and VR supports post-decision simulations, such as imagined usage scenarios.

2.5 A Summary of Selected Empirical Literature

To deepen the understanding of how VR has been employed for product and consumer research, Table 2.1 provides a structured overview of selected empirical studies. Extending Branca et al. (2023, 2024), the table summarizes the methodologies, product categories, experimental conditions, and main findings of the reviewed articles, highlighting key contributions to the field and offering a basis for the following analysis.

Most studies adopt experimental designs, often comparing VR conditions with physical stores or traditional online environments. Products tested range from food and beverages to apparel and durable goods, showing VR's versatility across categories. Findings highlight VR's ability to elicit realistic consumer behaviors, support cognitive and affective responses, and provide valuable insights into shopping processes and purchase intentions. At the same time, the results may be influenced by factors such as product type, consumer characteristics, and the level of immersion and interactivity offered.

2.6 Conclusions and Future Research Avenues

The existing literature on VR, product, and consumer research highlights several important trends and implications for both current and future research directions.

First, it emerges that the marketing and consumer behavior research communities are increasingly adopting VR, with significant growth observed particularly over the last years. Experimental methodology remains the dominant approach, confirming its suitability for studying complex cognitive, affective, and behavioral responses under controlled conditions. In particular, the growing use of VR HMDs is a notable trend. HMDs allow researchers to create highly immersive and interactive environments, strengthening the internal and ecological validity of laboratory experiments compared to more traditional screen-based or static simulations. Moreover, the increasing accessibility of VR technology among consumers (Deloitte,

Table 2.1 Selected literature on VR and product research

Authors	Methodology	Products	Conditions	Main findings
Kinzinger et al. (2025)	Laboratory experiment	Kitchen appliance	HTC Vive Pro HMD	Providing functional control alongside visual control in immersive VR webshops increases consumers' sense of presence, enjoyment, attitude toward shopping on the website, and purchase intention. The ability to interact with product functionalities enhances the hedonic shopping experience and reinforces behavioral intentions
Uysal et al. (2025)	Field experiment, laboratory experiment, qualitative interviews	Microwave, PlayStation, TV, bicycle, table	Oculus Rift S, Meta Quest 3, real products	VR product presentations benefit retailers when they showcase hedonic products, use interactive and realistic environments to rouse product imagination, show products in a congruent usage context, and allow virtual product assembly
Zhang et al. (2025)	Laboratory experiment	Shoes, slippers, outdoor camping chairs, storage boxes	Pico Neo 3, Meta Quest 2, desktop VR	Immersive VR is more effective than non-immersive VR when product interactivity is low, compensating for limited interaction. Under high interactivity, its advantage depends on product type and sensory design: it boosts purchase intention for graspable products, while for non-graspable products it is only superior if haptic cues are provided; without them, non-immersive VR is equally effective and more cost-efficient
Bigné et al. (2024)	Laboratory experiment, online survey	Snacks, sneakers	HTC VIVE Pro Eye, static picture displays	Semidurable goods require greater inspection and deliberation than fast-moving consumer goods. Visual inspection of the shelf and products was greater than a physical examination through virtual handling for both product categories
Zhang et al. (2024)	Laboratory experiment	Outdoor chair	Meta Quest 2 and Pico Neo 3, static pictures	VR retail environments enhance mental imagery and purchase intention compared to static images, but their effectiveness diminishes for consumers with high product knowledge. However, this negative effect is attenuated when consumers have an experiential shopping orientation or when evaluating high-involvement products

(continued)

Table 2.1 (continued)

Authors	Methodology	Products	Conditions	Main findings
Kim et al. (2022)	Laboratory experiment	Apparel	VR HMD, online store website	Compared to traditional website browsing, 360-degree VR store videos enhance consumers' flow states, which in turn boost their interest in the store and their intention to visit the physical location. Flow mediates the effect of VR experience on both outcomes, making VR an effective promotional tool for small retailers with limited resources
Luangrath et al. (2022)	Field study, online experiment, laboratory experiment	Coffee, knitting, electronics, shirts, sweater, t-shirts, blankets	Images, GIFs, Oculus Rift VR, real products	In VR retail settings, observing a virtual hand touching a product, rather than just viewing the product or a hand not in contact, enhances consumers' psychological ownership and increases product valuation. This vicarious haptic effect is stronger for individuals more stimulated by the immersive VR experience. Diagnostic touch movements are critical to trigger these effects
Alzayat and Lee (2021)	Laboratory experiment, online experiment	Tools, clothes	Oculus Rift, online retail website	Virtual touch in VR retail environments enhances hedonic shopping value compared to traditional online websites but does not improve utilitarian value. The type of product (extension vs. presentation of the body) influences consumer responses, with VR more suitable for products perceived as extensions of the body (compared to presentation of the body). Telepresence mediates the relationship between VR and shopping values
Cowan et al. (2021)	Field experiment, online experiment	Champagne, automobiles	360-VR, picture, video, real product, website video	360° VR retail experiences increase brand attitudes and purchase intentions when consumers interact remotely, compared to traditional video, but these outcomes may decrease when consumers are in-store. High-knowledge consumers show reduced brand responses in VR settings. Introducing haptic cues mitigates these negative effects. Mental imagery mediates the influence of VR presence on consumer outcome

(continued)

Table 2.1 (continued)

Authors	Methodology	Products	Conditions	Main findings
Harz et al. (2021)	Field study, laboratory experiment	Gardening tools	VR HMD, online VR, real product	VR simulations enhance consumer behavioral consistency between information search, preference formation, and purchase decisions compared to traditional studio tests with physical products. VR increases perceptions of presence and vividness, which drive forecast accuracy
Kang et al. (2020)	Online experiment, laboratory experiment	Office furniture	Picture, video desktop, website 3D video, Oculus Rift CV1	Interactivity and visual–spatial cues in 3D VR shopping environments enhance both perceived informativeness and playfulness. Playfulness increases preference for hedonic product attributes, while informativeness is the main driver of purchase intention. Graphics quality has less impact in VR than in 2D settings
Meißner et al. (2020)	Laboratory experiment	Muesli	VR HMD, desktop screen, real shelves	Compared to low-immersive environments, high-immersive VR shopping increases consumer variety-seeking and reduces price sensitivity, without significantly improving satisfaction with the choice made. High immersion does not enhance choice satisfaction
Naderi et al. (2020)	Laboratory experiment	Digital camera	Ultra-HD TV, Oculus Rift CV1	In VR settings, congruence between the product and environment enhances aesthetic perception and emotional responses, but has a limited effect on purchase intention
Schnack et al. (2020)	Laboratory experiment	Food and beverage	HTC Vive	Consumer behavior in an immersive VR store mirrors real-world shopping patterns
Pfeiffer et al. (2020)	Laboratory experiment, field study	Food and beverage	CAVE, eye-tracking, real products	Eye movement patterns in VR reflected those in physical stores, indicating strong external validity for VR consumer research
Pizzi et al. (2020)	Online experiment	Grocery store	Video in VR-based store, video in physical store	Consumers exposed to a VR retail environment reported higher levels of presence compared to a physical store. Enhanced presence improved the shopping experience, which strengthened value perceptions, leading to greater patronage intentions and WOM referral

(continued)

Table 2.1 (continued)

Authors	Methodology	Products	Conditions	Main findings
Martínez-Navarro et al. (2019)	Laboratory experiment, field experiment	Grocery store (beverage area)	Desktop screen, power-wall, HTC Vive, physical supermarket	VR supermarkets, particularly those experienced through HMDs, elicit higher brand recall and purchase intention, compared to physical stores. Purchase intention can vary according to VR configuration
Peukert et al. (2019)	Laboratory experiment	Muesli	HTC Vive, desktop computer screen	The effect of immersion on the intention to reuse the shopping environment operates through two pathways: one via perceived product diagnosticity and perceived usefulness, and the other via perceived telepresence and perceived enjoyment
Pizzi et al. (2019)	Quasi-experiment	Industrial confectionery	HTC Vive, physical store	VR produces comparable effects to the physical store in terms of shopping experience duration, as well as the type and number of products selected
Siegrist et al. (2019)	Laboratory experiment	Cereals	VR HMD, real shelf, real products	Consumer behaviors in a VR supermarket closely mirror those in physical stores, particularly for food product evaluation and selection
The present study	Laboratory experiment	Milk pack	Oculus Quest 2, real products	Consumers' response in terms of perceptions and attitudes, across three groups of packaging manipulations, show similar results between VR and PR

Source Author's elaboration on Branca et al. (2023, 2024)

2023; Flavián et al., 2019a) could reshape expectations for marketing research. As HMDs become more widespread in private and commercial use, there is a need to advance the understanding of consumer behavior in high-immersion, highly interactive environments.

Second, the field has seen growing studies in VR, but also comparisons between VR and other experimental conditions, including both online and offline settings. These works confirm the potential of VR not just as a novel consumer touchpoint, but as a credible substitute or complement to real-world research environments. However, previous literature also presents some mixed findings, since VR's outcomes seem not uniform across product categories, contexts, or measures, as in the case of utilitarian/hedonic products and experiences (e.g., Lee et al., 2025; Mishra et al., 2021) and purchase intention (e.g., Kang et al., 2020; Kim et al., 2022; Martínez-Navarro et al., 2019; Meißner et al., 2020; Pizzi et al., 2019, 2020). Pfeiffer et al. (2020) highlight some similarities between virtual and physical supermarkets, calling for research that contrasts VR with PR.

Third, VR has the potential to revolutionize shopping and retail, but also the product and packaging development process. Much of the research to date has taken a holistic perspective, analyzing consumer behavior in VR at the level of categories, shelves, or stores. While this provides important insights into shopping dynamics and store interactions, fewer studies have focused on a more analytical, attribute-specific evaluation of products within VR environments, and even fewer employ packaging. It is possible to identify some relevant examples, which have served as a reference for the development of this work and highlight some mixed findings. Among others, studies like Peukert et al. (2019) have found that product evaluation in VR closely resembles that in PR. In the realm of food products, VR provides realistic cues and drives natural product research (Huang et al., 2021). Studies found that consumers in a VR store exhibit similar shopping patterns and behaviors to those in PR, with minor differences in product evaluation (e.g., Huang et al., 2021; Schnack et al., 2020; Siegrist et al., 2019). Research should move toward more detailed investigations of how specific product features, such as packaging design and attributes, are perceived and evaluated in immersive settings. Indeed, consumer responses could produce different results if the focus of the study were an analytical feature of the product.

In summary, VR is gaining recognition as a valuable tool for studying consumer behavior and product evaluation. However, to better exploit its potential, research must move beyond broad analyses of shopping environments and focus more deeply on specific product attributes. In this perspective, packaging design represents a critical dimension of consumer evaluation, influencing perceptions, attitudes, and choices both in physical and virtual settings. An interesting gap emerging from this analysis is the intersection of immersive technology and sustainability. While VR is often discussed in terms of presence, interactivity, or consumer engagement, it also has significant environmental implications. Among other reasons, by replacing traditional product prototyping, VR can reduce resource consumption, minimize transportation needs, and accelerate the testing of packaging concepts. In this sense, immersive environments can serve as laboratories for exploring how consumers interpret analytical product attributes, such as packaging. Thus, sustainability cues and eco-design features can be tested in realistic store simulations, thereby helping firms align innovation processes with environmental regulations and consumer expectations. In conclusion, research should explicitly explore VR's potential also as a sustainability enabler, linking marketing to environmental goals. The next chapter explores the role of packaging design, with a particular focus on sustainability attributes, laying the foundation for the experimental investigation conducted in this research.

References

Alexander, B., Blazquez, M., Chrimes, C., & Boardman, R. (2025). The role of immersive spaces on the customer experience: An exploration of fashion metaverses. *Psychology & Marketing, 42*, 539–553. https://doi.org/10.1002/mar.22140

Alzayat, A., & Lee, S. H. M. (2021). Virtual products as an extension of my body: Exploring hedonic and utilitarian shopping value in a virtual reality retail environment. *Journal of Business Research, 130*, 348–363. https://doi.org/10.1016/j.jbusres.2021.03.017

Barnes, S. (2016). *Understanding virtual reality in marketing: Nature, implications*. https://ssrn.com/abstract=2909100

Berg, L. P., & Vance, J. M. (2017). Industry use of virtual reality in product design and manufacturing: A survey. *Virtual Reality, 21*(1), 1–17. https://doi.org/10.1007/s10055-016-0293-9

Bernritter, S. F., Ketelaar, P. E., & Sotgiu, F. (2021). Behaviorally targeted location-based mobile marketing. *Journal of the Academy of Marketing Science, 49*, 677–702. https://doi.org/10.1007/s11747-021-00784-0

Bigné, E., Llinares, C., & Torrecilla, C. (2016). Elapsed time on first buying triggers brand choices within a category: A virtual reality-based study. *Journal of Business Research, 69*(4), 1423–1427. https://doi.org/10.1016/j.jbusres.2015.10.119

Bigné, E., Simonetti, A., Guixeres, J., & Alcaniz, M. (2024). Visual attention and product interaction: A neuroscientific study on purchase across two product categories in a virtual store. *International Journal of Retail & Distribution Management, 52*(4), 389–406. https://doi.org/10.1108/IJRDM-02-2023-0067

Biocca, F., & Levy, M. R. (1995). *Communication in the Age of Virtual Reality*. Lawrence Erlbaum Associates.

Branca, G., Marino, V., & Resciniti, R. (2024). How do consumers evaluate products in virtual reality? A literature review for a research agenda. *Spanish Journal of Marketing—ESIC, 28*(3), 356–380. https://doi.org/10.1108/SJME-07-2022-0153

Branca, G., Resciniti, R., & Loureiro, S. M. C. (2023). Virtual is so real! Consumers' evaluation of product packaging in virtual reality. *Psychology & Marketing, 40*, 596–609. https://doi.org/10.1002/mar.21743

Bu, L., Chen, C. H., Ng, K. K. H., Zheng, P., Dong, G., & Liu, H. (2021). A user-centric design approach for smart product-service systems using virtual reality: A case study. *Journal of Cleaner Production, 280*(2), Article 124413. https://doi.org/10.1016/j.jclepro.2020.124413

Chen, H., Li, H., & Pirkkalainen, H. (2024). How extended reality influences e-commerce consumers: A literature review. *Electronic Commerce Research and Applications, 65*, Article 101404. https://doi.org/10.1016/j.elerap.2024.101404

Corallo, A., Lazoi, M., Papadia, G., & Pascarelli, C. (2020). Action research on Virtual-Reality-Assisted product and process design. *IEEE Transactions on Engineering Management*, 1-18. https://doi.org/10.1109/TEM.2020.3038461

Cowan, K., & Ketron, S. (2019a). A dual model of product involvement for effective virtual reality: The roles of imagination, co-creation, telepresence, and interactivity. *Journal of Business Research, 100*, 483–492. https://doi.org/10.1016/j.jbusres.2018.10.063

Cowan, K., & Ketron, S. (2019b). Prioritizing marketing research in virtual reality: Development of an immersion/fantasy typology. *European Journal of Marketing, 53*(8), 1585–1611. https://doi.org/10.1108/EJM-10-2017-0733

Cowan, K., Spielmann, N., Horn, E., & Griffart, C. (2021). Perception is reality… How digital retail environments influence brand perceptions through presence. *Journal of Business Research, 123*, 86–96. https://doi.org/10.1016/j.jbusres.2020.09.058

Deloitte. (2023). *Deloitte's 2023 Tech Trends report*. https://www.deloittedigital.com/au/en/insights/research/deloitte-tech-trends-report-2023.html

Dietrich, T., Rundle-Thiele, S., Kubacki, K., Durl, J., Gullo, M. J., Arli, D., & Connor, J. P. (2019). Virtual reality in social marketing: A process evaluation. *Marketing Intelligence & Planning, 37*(7), 806–820. https://doi.org/10.1108/MIP-11-2018-0537

Dwivedi, Y. K., Hughes, L., Baabdullah, A. M., Ribeiro-Navarrete, S., Giannakis, M., Al-Debei, M. M., Dennehy, D., Metri, B., Buhalis, D., Cheung, C. M., Conboy, K., Doyle, R., Dubey, R., Dutot, V., Felix, R., Goyal, D. P., Gustafsson, A., Hinsch, C., Jebabli, I., …, Wamba, S. F. (2022). Metaverse beyond the hype: Multidisciplinary perspectives on emerging challenges, opportunities, and agenda for research, practice and policy. *International Journal of Information Management, 66*, 102542. https://doi.org/10.1016/j.ijinfomgt.2022.102542

Esmark Jones, C. L., Barney, C., & Farmer, A. (2018). Appreciating anonymity: An exploration of embarrassing products and the power of blending in. *Journal of Retailing, 94*(2), 186–202. https://doi.org/10.1016/j.jretai.2018.01.001

Fares, O. H., Aversa, J., Lee, S. H., & Jacobson, J. (2024). Virtual reality: A review and a new framework for integrated adoption. *International Journal of Consumer Studies, 48*(2), Article e13040. https://doi.org/10.1111/ijcs.13040

Flavián, C., Ibáñez-Sánchez, S., & Orús, C. (2019a). Integrating virtual reality devices into the body: Effects of technological embodiment on customer engagement and behavioral intentions toward the destination. *Journal of Travel and Tourism Marketing, 36*(7), 847–863. https://doi.org/10.1080/10548408.2019.1618781

Flavián, C., Ibáñez-Sánchez, S., & Orús, C. (2019b). The impact of virtual, augmented and mixed reality technologies on the customer experience. *Journal of Business Research, 100*, 547–560. https://doi.org/10.1016/j.jbusres.2018.10.050

Flavián, C., Ibáñez-Sánchez, S., & Orús, C. (2021). Impacts of technological embodiment through virtual reality on potential guests' emotions and engagement. *Journal of Hospitality Marketing and Management, 30*(1), 1–20. https://doi.org/10.1080/19368623.2020.1770146

Guttentag, D. (2010). Virtual reality: Applications and implications for tourism. *Tourism Management, 31*(5), 637–651. https://doi.org/10.1016/j.tourman.2009.07.003

Han, S. L., An, M., Han, J. J., & Lee, J. (2020). Telepresence, time distortion, and consumer traits of virtual reality shopping. *Journal of Business Research, 118*, 311–320. https://doi.org/10.1016/j.jbusres.2020.06.056

Harz, N., Hohenberg, S., & Homburg, C. (2021). Virtual reality in new product development: Insights from pre-launch sales forecasting for durables. *Journal of Marketing*, 1–23. https://doi.org/10.1177/00222429211014902

Heller, J., Chylinski, M., de Ruyter, K., Keeling, D. I., Hilken, T., & Mahr, D. (2021). Tangible service automation: Decomposing the technology-enabled engagement process (TEEP) for augmented reality. *Journal of Service Research, 24*(1), 84–103. https://doi.org/10.1177/1094670520933692

Hilken, T., Chylinski, M., Keeling, D. I., Heller, J., Ruyter, K., & Mahr, D. (2022). How to strategically choose or combine augmented and virtual reality for improved online experiential retailing. *Psychology & Marketing, 39*, 495–507. https://doi.org/10.1002/mar.21600

Hollebeek, L. D., Clark, M. K., Andreassen, T. W., Sigurdsson, V., & Smith, D. (2020). Virtual reality through the customer journey: Framework and propositions. *Journal of Retailing and Consumer Services, 55*, Article 102056. https://doi.org/10.1016/j.jretconser.2020.102056

Hoyer, W. D., Kroschke, M., Schmitt, B., Kraume, K., & Shankar, V. (2020). Transforming the customer experience through new technologies. *Journal of Interactive Marketing, 51*, 57–71. https://doi.org/10.1016/j.intmar.2020.04.001

Huang, J., & Wan, X. (2019). The color–flavor incongruency effect in product evaluation and brand perception. *Journal of Consumer Behaviour, 18*, 484–495. https://doi.org/10.1002/cb.1787

Huang, J., Zhao, P., & Wan, X. (2021). From brain variations to individual differences in the color–flavor incongruency effect: A combined virtual reality and resting-state fMRI study. *Journal of Business Research, 123*, 604–612. https://doi.org/10.1016/j.jbusres.2020.10.031

Hube, N., Müller, M., Lapczyna, E., & Wojdziak, J. (2020). Mixed Reality based collaboration for design processes. *i-com, 19*(2), 123–137. https://doi.org/10.1515/icom-2020-0012.

Kang, H. J., Shin, J., & Ponto, K. (2020). How 3D Virtual Reality stores can shape consumer purchase decisions: The roles of informativeness and playfulness. *Journal of Interactive Marketing, 49*, 70–85. https://doi.org/10.1016/j.intmar.2019.07.002

Ketelaar, P. E., Bernritter, S. F., van Woudenberg, T. J., Rozendaal, E., Konig, R. P., Hühn, A. E., Van Gisbergen, M. S., & Janssen, L. (2018). Opening' location-based mobile ads: How openness and location congruency of location-based ads weaken negative effects of intrusiveness on brand choice. *Journal of Business Research, 91*, 277–285. https://doi.org/10.1016/j.jbusres.2018.06.018

Ketelaar, P. E., Bernritter, S. F., van't Riet, J., Hühn, A. E., van Woudenberg, T. J., Müller, B. C. N., & Janssen, L. (2017). Disentangling location-based advertising: The effects of location congruency and medium type on consumers' ad attention and brand choice. *International Journal of Advertising, 36*(2), 356–367. https://doi.org/10.1080/02650487.2015.1093810.

Kim, G., Jin, B., & Shin, D. C. (2022). Virtual reality as a promotion tool for small independent stores. *Journal of Retailing and Consumer Services, 64*, Article 102822. https://doi.org/10.1016/j.jretconser.2021.102822

Kim, J.-H., Kim, M., Park, M., & Yoo, J. (2021). How interactivity and vividness influence consumer virtual reality shopping experience: The mediating role of telepresence. *Journal of Research in Interactive Marketing, 15*(3), 502–525. https://doi.org/10.1108/JRIM-07-2020-0148

Kinzinger, A., Steiner, W. J., Tatzgern, M., & Vallaster, C. (2025). Interactive product presentation in an immersive environment: The influence of functional control on hedonic aspects. *Journal of Retailing and Consumer Services, 83*, Article 104156. https://doi.org/10.1016/j.jretconser.2024.104156

Krueger, M. (1991). *Artificial Reality II*. Addison-Wesley Professional.

LaValle, S. M. (2017). *Virtual reality*. Cambridge University Press.

Lee, M., Lee, S. A., Jeong, M., & Oh, H. (2020). Quality of virtual reality and its impacts on behavioral intention. *International Journal of Hospitality Management, 90*, Article 102595. https://doi.org/10.1016/j.ijhm.2020.102595

Lee, S., Choi, K., & Kim, M. (2025). Engaging consumers with Virtual Reality: A moderation role of product types and consumption orientations. *Psychology & Marketing, 42*, 655–668. https://doi.org/10.1002/mar.22144

Lombart, C., Millan, E., Normand, J. M., Verhulst, A., Labbé-Pinlon, B., & Moreau, G. (2019). Consumer perceptions and purchase behavior toward imperfect fruits and vegetables in an immersive virtual reality grocery store. *Journal of Retailing and Consumer Services, 48*, 28–40. https://doi.org/10.1016/j.jretconser.2019.01.010

Luangrath, A. W., Peck, J., Hedgcock, W., & Xu, Y. (2022). Observing product touch: The vicarious haptic effect in digital marketing and virtual reality. *Journal of Marketing Research, 59*(2), 306–326. https://doi.org/10.1177/00222437211059540

Loureiro, S. M. C., Guerreiro, J., & Japutra, A. (2021). How escapism leads to behavioral intention in a virtual reality store with background music? *Journal of Business Research, 134*, 288–300. https://doi.org/10.1016/j.jbusres.2021.05.035

Loureiro, S. M. C., Guerreiro, J., Eloy, E., Langaro, D., & Panchapakesan, P. (2019). Understanding the use of Virtual Reality in Marketing: A text mining-based review. *Journal of Business Research, 100*, 514–530. https://doi.org/10.1016/j.jbusres.2018.10.055

Luna-Nevarez, C., & McGovern, E. (2021). The rise of the virtual reality (VR) marketplace: Exploring the antecedents and consequences of consumer attitudes toward V-Commerce. *Journal of Internet Commerce, 20*(2), 167–194. https://doi.org/10.1080/15332861.2021.1875766

Martínez-Navarro, J., Bigné, E., Guixeres, J., Alcañiz, M., & Torrecilla, C. (2019). The influence of virtual reality in e-commerce. *Journal of Business Research, 100*, 475–482. https://doi.org/10.1016/j.jbusres.2018.10.054

Marx, T., Welle, G., & Gier-Reinartz, N. R. (2025). Enhancing virtual reality experiences in grocery retailing: the impact of audio priming on spatial presence and retailer outcomes. *The International Review of Retail, Distribution and Consumer Research*, 1–25. https://doi.org/10.1080/09593969.2025.2512303

Meißner, M., Pfeiffer, J., Peukert, C., Dietrich, H., & Pfeiffer, T. (2020). How virtual reality affects consumer choice. *Journal of Business Research, 117*, 219–231. https://doi.org/10.1016/j.jbusres.2020.06.004

Meißner, M., Pfeiffer, J., Pfeiffer, T., & Oppewal, H. (2019). Combining virtual reality and mobile eye tracking to provide a naturalistic experimental environment for shopper research. *Journal of Business Research, 100*, 445–458. https://doi.org/10.1016/j.jbusres.2017.09.028

Milgram, P., & Kishino, F. (1994). A taxonomy of mixed reality visual displays. *IEICE Transactions on Information and Systems, 77*(12), 1321–1329.

Milgram, P., Takemura, H., Utsumi, A., & Kishino, F. (1994). Augmented reality: A class of displays on the reality-virtuality continuum. Systems research. In H. Das (Ed.), *Telemanipulator and telepresence technologies* (Vol. 2351, pp. 282–292). Photonics for Industrial Applications. https://doi.org/10.1117/12.197321

Mishra, A., Shukla, A., Rana, N. P., & Dwivedi, Y. K. (2021). From "touch" to a "multisensory" experience: The impact of technology interface and product type on consumer responses. *Psychology & Marketing, 38*, 385–396. https://doi.org/10.1002/mar.21436

Naderi, E., Naderi, I., & Balakrishnan, B. (2020). Product design matters, but is it enough? Consumers' responses to product design and environment congruence. *Journal of Product & Brand Management, 29*(7), 939–954. https://doi.org/10.1108/JPBM-08-2018-1975

Orús, C., Ibáñez-Sánchez, S., & Flavián, C. (2021). Enhancing the customer experience with virtual and augmented reality: The impact of content and device type. *International Journal of Hospitality Management, 98*, Article 103019. https://doi.org/10.1016/j.ijhm.2021.103019

Pala, E., Kapitan, S., & Esch, P. (2021). Simulated satiation through reality-enhancing technology. *Psychology & Marketing, 39*, 483–494. https://doi.org/10.1002/mar.21582

Park, H., & Kim, S. (2021). Do augmented and virtual reality technologies increase consumers' purchase intentions? The role of cognitive elaboration and shopping goals. *Clothing and Textiles Research Journal, 41*(2). https://doi.org/10.1177/0887302X21994287

Peukert, C., Pfeiffer, J., Meißner, M., Pfeiffer, T., & Weinhardt, C. (2019). Shopping in Virtual Reality stores: The influence of immersion on system adoption. *Journal of Management Information Systems, 36*(3), 755–788. https://doi.org/10.1080/07421222.2019.1628889

Pfeiffer, P., Pfeiffer, T., Meißner, M., & Weiß, E. (2020). Eye-Tracking-based classification of information search behavior using Machine Learning: Evidence from experiments in physical shops and Virtual Reality shopping environments. *Information Systems Research, 31*(3), 675–691. https://doi.org/10.1287/isre.2019.0907

Pizzi, G., Scarpi, D., Pichierri, M., & Vannucci, V. (2019). Virtual reality, real reactions?: Comparing consumers' perceptions and shopping orientation across physical and virtual-reality retail stores. *Computers in Human Behavior, 96*, 1–12. https://doi.org/10.1016/j.chb.2019.02.008

Pizzi, G., Vannucci, V., & Aiello, G. (2020). Branding in the time of virtual reality: Are virtual store brand perceptions real? *Journal of Business Research, 119*, 502–510. https://doi.org/10.1016/j.jbusres.2019.11.063

PwC. (2019). *Seeing is believing.* How Virtual Reality and Augmented Reality are transforming business and the economy. https://www.pwc.com/gx/en/technology/publications/assets/how-virtual-reality-and-augmented-reality.pdf

Ringler, C., Sirianni, N. J., & Christenson, B. (2021). The power of consequential product sounds. *Journal of Retailing, 97*(2), 288–300. https://doi.org/10.1016/j.jretai.2020.09.002

Rodrigues, M. B., & Loureiro, S. M. C. (2022). Virtual reality in the motion picture industry: The relationship among movie coolness, sympathy, empathy, and word-of-mouth. *Journal of Promotion Management, 28*(2), 144–159. https://doi.org/10.1080/10496491.2021.1987964

Schnack, A., Wright, M. J., & Elms, J. (2021a). Investigating the impact of shopper personality on behaviour in immersive Virtual Reality store environments. *Journal of Retailing and Consumer Services, 61*, Article 102581. https://doi.org/10.1016/j.jretconser.2021.102581

Schnack, A., Wright, J. M., & Holdershaw, J. L. (2021b). Does the locomotion technique matter in an immersive virtual store environment?—Comparing motion-tracked walking and instant teleportation. *Journal of Retailing and Consumer Services, 58*, Article 102266. https://doi.org/10.1016/j.jretconser.2020.102266

Schnack, A., Wright, M. J., & Holdershaw, J. L. (2020). An exploratory investigation of shopper behaviour in an immersive virtual reality store. *Journal of Consumer Behaviour, 19*, 182–195. https://doi.org/10.1002/cb.1803

Sherman, W. R., & Craig, A. B. (2002). *Understanding virtual reality: Interface, application, and design.* Morgan Kaufmann Publishers Inc.

Siegrist, M., Ung, C.-Y., Zank, M., Marinello, M., Kunz, A., Hartmann, C., & Menozzi, M. (2019). Consumers' food selection behaviors in three-dimensional (3D) virtual reality. *Food Research International, 117*, 50–59. https://doi.org/10.1016/j.foodres.2018.02.033

Statista (2024). *Virtual reality (VR)—Statistics & facts.* https://www.statista.com/topics/2532/virtual-reality-vr/#topicOverview

Uysal, E., Finken, D., Krämer, M., Alavi, S., Jun, Y., & Schendzielarz, D. (2025). Virtually mine: Understanding consumer responses to virtual reality product presentations. *Journal of Retailing.* https://doi.org/10.1016/j.jretai.2025.04.007

van Berlo, Z. M. C., van Reijmersdal, E. A., Smit, E. G., & van der Laan, L. N. (2021). Brands in virtual reality games: Affective processes within computer-mediated consumer experiences. *Journal of Business Research, 122*, 458–465. https://doi.org/10.1016/j.jbusres.2020.09.006

Wedel, M., Bigné, E., & Zhang, J. (2020). Virtual and augmented reality: Advancing research in consumer marketing. *International Journal of Research in Marketing, 37*(3), 443–465. https://doi.org/10.1016/j.ijresmar.2020.04.004

Xi, N., & Hamari, J. (2021). Shopping in virtual reality: A literature review and future agenda. *Journal of Business Research, 134*, 37–58. https://doi.org/10.1016/j.jbusres.2021.04.075

Zhang, Y., Shao, W., Quach, S., Thaichon, P., & Li, Q. (2024). Examining the moderating effects of shopping orientation, product knowledge and involvement on the effectiveness of Virtual Reality (VR) retail environment. *Journal of Retailing and Consumer Services, 78*, Article 103713. https://doi.org/10.1016/j.jretconser.2024.103713

Zhang, Y., Shao, W., Quach, S., Thaichon, P., & Li, Q. (2025). VR retailing: When and why immersion pays off. *Journal of Retailing.* https://doi.org/10.1016/j.jretai.2025.04.004

Chapter 3
Packaging Design, Sustainability and the Consumer Perspective

3.1 Packaging Role in Consumers' Choices

Packaging is a multifaceted element that extends beyond its role as a container for products and how items are wrapped and presented to consumers in retail settings (Herédia-Colaço, 2023; Park & Ma, 2019). It represents a strategic factor in the marketing mix. It possesses functional attributes, but also the power to convey information and influence consumers' product evaluations, preferences, and choices, making it a critical factor in in-store purchase decisions (Liao et al., 2015). Sometimes called a tacit salesperson (Baruk & Iwanicka, 2015), packaging is often the first element to which retail shoppers are exposed when choosing from alternatives on stores' shelves. Consumers first encounter the packaging of a product itself, and they use package features as cues to appraise the product. Remarkably, some companies spend more on packaging than advertising (Söderlund et al., 2017).

Packaging includes several features that characterize the visual appearance of the product (Herédia-Colaço, 2023) and serves as a potent communication tool (Park & Ma, 2019), allowing complete control of the information displayed (e.g., Du et al., 2010; Gofman et al., 2010; Monnot et al., 2019; Orth & De Marchi, 2007; Wei et al., 2018). By attracting the gaze and attention of the consumer, packaging influences customer decision-making (Aday & Yener, 2014; Chandon, 2013; Eberhart & Naderer, 2017; Monnot et al., 2015). Once attended, claims presented on the packaging are considered more reliable than those in an advertisement (Fajardo & Townsend, 2016). It instigates desire and facilitates product sales (Briand Decré & Cloonan, 2019). Indeed, packaging design can effectively communicate product attributes and brand values and elicit consumer response (Festila & Chrysochou, 2018). Packaging plays a role in shaping in-store purchase decisions as consumers often rely on its features to evaluate products, even without seeing the actual item (Holmes & Paswan, 2012; Söderlund et al., 2017). Packaging can affect consumers' attitudes toward the product, their quality assessment, and value perception (e.g., Chen, 2021; Coelho do Vale & Verga Matos, 2015; Park & Ma, 2019). Through its

G. Branca, *Virtual Reality, Real Intentions*, International Series in Advanced Management Studies, https://doi.org/10.1007/978-3-032-10142-6_3

graphical, textual, and structural design elements, packaging can enhance product attributes. In the end, packaging characteristics affect how consumers evaluate and choose the products (Coelho do Vale & Verga Matos, 2015).

The significance of packaging design cannot be underestimated when it comes to determining a product's success. It serves to not only showcase the product but also to differentiate it from competitors. Effective packaging design conveys information, provides sensory stimulation, and captivates (Holmes & Paswan, 2012; Liao et al., 2015). A salient packaging design element has the potential to effectively influence product evaluations and consumer responses. Consequently, packaging design emerges as a strategic asset for enhancing business competitiveness, a point underscored by various scholars who emphasize its relevance in brand differentiation (e.g., Canto Primo et al., 2021; Qiao & Griffin, 2022).

In previous literature, two main approaches could be identified (Chrysochou & Festila, 2019). First, following a holistic approach, consumers' evaluation is elicited by the overall appearance of the packaging, with responses arising from the combination of all packaging elements. The second approach is based on an analytical or atomistic perspective and considers the individual elements that compose a packaging, looking at them in isolation. According to cue utilization theory (Olson, 1978), products and packaging offer multiple cues that consumers rely on to evaluate products. These cues are gathered and processed to guide their purchasing decisions (Hwang & Kim, 2022). Indeed, packaging can be intended as a series of design elements that serve as cues for consumers (Steenis et al., 2017).

This research builds on the analytical approach, treating package design elements separately, in line with previous contributions (e.g., Aagerup et al., 2019; Chrysochou & Festila, 2019; Festila & Chrysochou, 2018; Gosselt et al., 2019; Monnot et al., 2019). This approach allows us to gain a more comprehensive understanding of consumer responses to packaging by analyzing different isolated cues. Depending on their nature, these cues may yield varying responses. As an example, literature has identified concrete packaging attributes that influence consumers' response, such as color, texture, and shape (Söderlund et al., 2017), and focused on consumers' assessment and perception of packaging elements, such as material, shape, and logos (Herbes et al., 2020; Nguyen et al., 2020).

3.2 Packaging Design Elements

When it comes to packaging design elements, several classifications may be identified in previous literature. Magnier and Crié (2015) propose three categories of cues:

(a) structural ones (e.g., size, shape, materials);
(b) graphical cues (e.g., colors, photographs, images, logos);
(c) informational cues (e.g., labels, claims).

Festila and Chrysochou (2018) categorize packaging design elements as:

(a) informational (e.g., claims, labels);
(b) graphic (e.g., colors, imagery, typeface);
(c) structural (e.g., shape, size, material).

According to Herédia-Colaço (2023), packaging cues can be divided into:

(a) graphic ones (e.g., color, typeface, logos);
(b) structural ones (e.g., shape, size, material).

To find a synthesis in the previous literature and identify relevant packaging cues belonging to the different categorizations, we can start by focusing on some of the most representative ones, such as packaging material (structural), texture (haptic) and color (visual).

First, packaging material refers to the material a package is made of (e.g., plastic, glass, carton, or metal). Its choice depends on factors such as product type, logistic conditions, cost, storage, and protection requisites, and the values it is associated with (Chrysochou & Festila, 2019). Consumers use packaging material to make inferences about the product (Festila & Chrysochou, 2018). A significant proportion of research on packaging material concerns sustainability since consumers generally rely on packaging material to assess its eco-friendliness (Nguyen et al., 2020), as later detailed.

Second, packaging finishes have attracted researchers' attention only recently (Chen, 2021), as haptic was usually less studied among the senses in marketing research (Littel & Orth, 2013). Packaging texture needs more attention since there is a paucity of research in the literature (Briand Decré & Cloonan, 2019). Consumers can use the haptic sense to generate input by touching and handling the packaging (Festila & Chrysochou, 2018). Touch comprises three dimensions, namely cutaneous, kinesthetic, and haptic. The latter combines the cutaneous and kinesthetic dimensions of touch and is associated with the active touch (Briand Decré & Cloonan, 2019). Among others, Chen (2021) highlights that the difference between matte and glossy packaging depends on the touch and feel using hands, and how the light reflects. Matte surfaces are rough and soft, reflections of light are more diffuse and distributed in a wide range of directions, whereas glossy surfaces are smooth and hard and have single-angle light reflections. Matte packaging elicits stronger consumer evaluation and purchase intention than glossy packaging (Chen, 2021).

Third, color is one of the most important elements of packaging design, since it is a relevant source of package differentiation, grasping consumer attention, eliciting emotions and conveying values (Chrysochou & Festila, 2019; Marozzo et al., 2020). Color affects consumer response in several contexts (Festila & Chrysochou, 2018; Liao et al., 2015) and can recall specific images in consumers' minds, playing a role in the decision-making process (Ku & Chen, 2023). Previous research shows that different packaging colors can influence consumers' perceptions (Marozzo et al., 2020).

3.3 Packaging and Sustainability

Environmental sustainability is among the most salient challenges society is confronting in this historical period. Media and literature place increasing attention on concepts like sustainable development. Growing concern about sustainability from social actors has influenced consumption behaviors and translated into more awareness and more desire for responsible choices (Resciniti, 2020). Sustainability is an opportunity to pursue benefits for society and business. Marketing has the potential to influence sustainable lifestyles and promote sustainable products (Kemper & Ballantine, 2019).

Waste production has been a significant environmental issue in recent years (Hoornweg & Bhada-Tata, 2012). A third of pollution comes from packaging used in daily consumption, especially for food products (Herbes et al., 2020). Even if packaging fulfills many essential functions, the sustainability of packaging production is a matter of scrutiny. Companies are led to adopt sustainable practices in their activities and, consequently, to opt for eco-friendly packaging or green packaging (Ferrara et al., 2020; Prakash et al., 2019).

Eco-friendly packaging can potentially contribute to sustainable development (Lindh et al., 2016a; Nguyen et al., 2020; Wikström et al., 2018). However, both companies and consumers are confused about what makes packaging sustainable (Ertz et al., 2017; Jerzyk, 2016; Nguyen et al., 2020). Overlooking the issue of sustainability related to packaging may lead to underestimating an important aspect.

According to Zeng and Durif (2020), a definition of eco-friendly packaging can be reached from two perspectives: from an engineering point of view (Steenis et al., 2017), it refers to the actual environmental impact according to life cycle assessment (LCA); while from a consumers' perspective, sustainable packaging involves consumer perceptions that a design explicitly or implicitly evokes eco-friendliness (Magnier et al., 2016). A similar classification was also presented by Magnier and Crié (2015), moving from a previous framework proposed by Boks and Stevels (2007). According to the authors, eco-friendliness can be identified in three categories:

(a) scientific, referring to the life cycle of the product;
(b) governmental, referring to legal requirements; and
(c) consumer, referring to the perception of individuals.

There are also technical definitions of sustainable packaging (Herbes et al., 2018, 2020; Jerzyk, 2016; Lindh et al., 2016b; Nguyen et al., 2020; Scott & Vigar-Ellis, 2014). One was provided in 2007 by the Sustainable Packaging Alliance (SPA) and is based on four sustainability principles that packaging should meet:

(a) effective, providing social and economic benefits:
(b) efficient, providing benefits by using materials, energy, and water as efficiently as possible;
(c) cyclic, being recoverable through industrial or natural systems; and
(d) safe, i.e., non-polluting and non-toxic.

A different definition was promoted by the Sustainable Packaging Coalition (SPC) in 2011. It was claimed that sustainable packaging must respect at least eight requirements, i.e., it:

(a) is beneficial, safe, and healthy for individuals and communities throughout its life cycle;
(b) meets market criteria for performance and cost;
(c) is sourced, manufactured, transported, and recycled using renewable energy;
(d) optimizes the use of renewable or recycled source materials;
(e) is manufactured using clean production technologies and best practices;
(f) is made from materials healthy throughout the life cycle;
(g) is physically designed to optimize materials and energy;
(h) is effectively recovered and utilized in biological and/or industrial closed-loop cycles.

Eco-friendly packaging supports consumers' desire to make responsible choices, but it is crucial to understand how consumers define and recognize eco-friendly attributes. Consequently, to address the growing relevance of sustainability in packaging design and consumer behavior, this chapter presents a comprehensive review of academic contributions focused on green packaging, building on Branca et al. (2024). The review compiles and organizes the eco-friendly attributes and sustainability cues of packaging that have been analyzed and evaluated in the consumer domain. The objective is to offer a clear and structured overview of design strategies aimed at presenting packaging sustainability and communicating environmental friendliness.

3.4 Previous Frameworks and Conceptualizations

3.4.1 Reviews on Packaging and Sustainability

Several literature reviews have examined the interplay between packaging and sustainability, each contributing distinct insights. A synthesis is presented in Table 3.1, building on and extending Branca et al. (2024). Bangsa and Schlegelmilch (2020) provided a broad overview of sustainable product attributes, including packaging, showing that while packaging is a key driver of consumer decision-making, it is often addressed only marginally and lacks focused conceptual development. Molina-Besch (2016) reviewed food LCAs and proposed guidelines for green packaging prioritization, focusing primarily on minimizing food waste and household energy consumption. Adding on this, Brennan et al. (2021) offered a systematized review of packaging's role in reducing household food waste, revealing that consumers often misunderstand the sustainability role of packaging, especially about food preservation functions. Ketelsen et al. (2020) focused on environmentally friendly food packaging and highlighted the main barriers to consumer adoption, such as low recognizability of sustainable packaging, lack of knowledge, and competing product priorities, while calling for better design communication. Zeng et al. (2020) conducted an epistemological review of eco-design packaging literature and stressed the need for transformative, consumer-centric research that incorporates social impacts and behavioral change. Afif et al. (2022) developed a framework focused on the drivers, barriers, and performance outcomes of sustainable packaging adoption, primarily from a supply chain and firm perspective, with a lower emphasis on consumer-facing design elements. Akturan et al. (2025) mapped 27 years of literature in marketing and consumer behavior on packaging and identified packaging sustainability as one of several themes. Eco-friendly packaging cues, such as labels, colors, claims, and material types, can influence consumer perceptions, attitudes, and behaviors, but these effects may be context-dependent and vary across studies. Baskoro et al. (2024) explored communication barriers around bioplastic packaging and highlighted the importance of credible labeling and signal clarity to support consumer understanding and proper disposal. Lau and Wong (2024) synthesized multidisciplinary studies and identified four major domains, materials, management, consumer behavior, and waste, stressing the fragmented nature of existing knowledge and the need for integrated strategies.

While these reviews have provided valuable overviews, they tend to treat sustainable packaging either broadly or from a technical or managerial standpoint. Few of them focus in depth on packaging sustainability through concrete, design-level attributes. In this context, this chapter, which builds on Branca et al. (2024), contributes to the literature by systematically categorizing sustainability-related packaging cues and detailing their effects on consumer perceptions and behaviors. This analytical focus addresses the existing literature by organizing fragmented insights into a comprehensive framework grounded in consumer response, enabling a more precise understanding of how packaging design supports or hinders sustainability.

3.4.2 *Main Research Directions in the Sustainable Packaging Marketing Literature*

As reported in Branca et al. (2024), Steenis et al. (2017) showed that prior research on consumer responses to eco-friendly packaging can be grouped into three main streams: (a) general attitudinal models; (b) holistic approaches; and (c) analytical approaches. The first stream emphasizes consumers' general willingness to adopt green packaging but provides less insight into the influence of specific packaging attributes on eco-friendliness evaluations. The second stream, the holistic perspective, explores the broader concept of eco-friendly packaging, offering an overall understanding from the consumer's point of view, even though detailed examinations of specific packaging characteristics are often lacking. The third stream adopts an

Table 3.1 Selected previous reviews on packaging and sustainability

Authors	Methodology	Purpose	Context	Main findings
Akturan et al. (2025)	Systematic literature review, 143 articles	Offer a comprehensive synthesis of 27 years of packaging literature in the marketing and consumer behavior fields	Packaging	The article proposes seven core themes: package format; package features; package sustainability; package label; package perception; package experience; package redesign
Baskoro et al. (2024)	Systematic literature review, 68 articles	Investigate communication processes, barriers, and mechanisms that influence consumer adoption and disposal behavior of bioplastic packaging	Bioplastic packaging	Bioplastic packaging can be a sustainable alternative to conventional plastic. The article emphasizes the importance of effective communication to improve consumer understanding and behavior
Branca et al. (2024)	Systematic literature review, 52 articles	Synthesize existing academic contributions on eco-friendly packaging design within the consumer behavior domain. Classify sustainability attributes and packaging cues	Sustainable packaging	The article identifies four main themes: consumers' knowledge and understanding of sustainable packaging; studies that investigate green packaging following a holistic approach; studies employing an analytical approach to identifying relevant package cues; and consumers' attitudes and behaviors toward eco-friendly packaging
Lau and Wong (2024)	Systematic literature review, 419 articles	Consolidate fragmented research on sustainable packaging across disciplines and provide a structured overview of major domains	Sustainable packaging	The main research domains are: sustainable packaging materials and properties; management practices of sustainable packaging; consumer behaviors toward sustainable packaging; packaging waste management. Consumers' responses are influenced by attitudes, knowledge, price, functionality, and design cues

(continued)

Table 3.1 (continued)

Authors	Methodology	Purpose	Context	Main findings
Afif et al. (2022)	Systematic literature review, 48 articles	Provide a comprehensive overview of the drivers, barriers, and performance outcomes of sustainable packaging	Sustainable packaging	The main key drivers are: the integrative and collaborative supply chain; environmental capabilities and resources; market-based instruments; cost reduction; consumer pressure; competitive advantage; regulatory pressure. The main barriers are: cost/benefit ambiguity; additional costs; complex trade-offs between packaging requirements. Sustainable packaging often improves environmental, social, and economic performance. To improve sustainability, packaging decisions should be integrated at three levels: vertical and horizontal integration; upstream and downstream integration; product-packaging integration
Brennan et al. (2021)	Systematic literature review, 345 items	Investigate consumer perceptions and behavior related to food packaging and household food waste	Food packaging	Packaging is framed as a functional tool in sustainability efforts. Food packaging can reduce household food waste by improving food protection, extending shelf life, providing appropriate portion sizes, and enhancing communication
Bangsa and Schlegelmilch (2020)	Systematic literature review, 93 articles	Analyze the relationship between sustainable product attributes and consumer decision-making	Sustainable products	The article includes packaging as one of the sustainability attributes through which environmental and social sustainability are communicated to consumers

(continued)

Table 3.1 (continued)

Authors	Methodology	Purpose	Context	Main findings
Ketelsen et al. (2020)	Systematic literature review, 46 articles	Analyze the state of the art on consumer responses to eco-friendly food packaging, identify barriers to purchase, and suggest ways to overcome them	Food packaging	Consumers often struggle to recognize eco-friendly packaging and lack sufficient knowledge, leading to a gap between positive attitudes and actual purchase behavior. Overcoming these barriers requires clearer sustainability cues, consumer education, and alignment with valued product attributes
Molina-Besch (2016)	Systematic literature review, 47 articles	Prioritization guidelines for green food packaging development by analyzing the role and impact of packaging throughout food supply chains, based on the findings from food Life Cycle Assessments (LCAs)	Green food packaging	Packaging's contribution to environmental impact is generally low compared to primary production, except for products packaged in heavy materials (e.g., glass, metal). Prioritization should consider: minimizing food waste; reducing household energy use; optimizing packaging material

Source Author's elaboration on Branca et al. (2024)

atomistic and analytical focus, investigating the effects of packaging cues by isolating particular elements and examining their individual impact on consumer perceptions and behavior. Building on this framework, the following sections are structured accordingly. First, an analysis of consumers' general knowledge and understanding of eco-friendly packaging it is presented, followed by studies adopting a holistic approach. Next, contributions applying an analytical perspective are discussed, including the differentiation of packaging cues based on their nature, drawing from classifications proposed in prior literature (Branca et al., 2024; Herbes et al., 2020; Magnier & Crié, 2015). Finally, an overview of research addressing consumers' attitudes and behaviors toward green packaging is provided, with reference to earlier reviews (e.g., Ketelsen et al., 2020).

3.5 Consumer Knowledge and Perceptions of Eco-Friendly Packaging

Despite growing environmental awareness, consumer understanding of what constitutes sustainable packaging remains limited and often confused (Jerzyk, 2016; Nguyen et al., 2020). A frequent theme in the literature is the need to clarify what sustainable packaging means from the consumer's perspective. Eco-friendly packaging, as perceived by consumers, can either explicitly or implicitly evoke sustainability through its structure, graphic elements, or informational content (Magnier & Crié, 2015; Magnier et al., 2016). Magnier and Crié (2015) applied a cost–benefit approach to categorize consumer perceptions of ecological packaging cues, distinguishing private benefits (such as health, convenience, lower price, and emotional value) and pro-social benefits (like environmental protection and societal well-being). Meanwhile, perceived costs included the loss of pleasure during the consumption experience, aesthetic costs, reduced product quality, hygiene concerns, decreased functionality, and higher prices.

Nguyen et al. (2020) further identified three main dimensions shaping consumers' perceptions of green packaging in Vietnam: packaging materials (e.g., biodegradable, non-toxic, recyclable, paper-based, decomposable); eco-friendly production processes (e.g., organic and natural materials, low environmental impact); and market appeal (e.g., attractive design, performance, pricing). Other studies support these findings in different contexts. In South Africa, eco-friendly packaging was associated with non-harmful, biodegradable, recyclable materials, reusability, and green manufacturing process (Scott & Vigar-Ellis, 2014). Venter et al. (2011) noted that South African consumers placed emphasis on functional and physical attributes like recyclability, quality, and hygiene when assessing packaging. In contrast, Jerzyk (2016) found moderate familiarity with sustainable packaging and relatively low importance in the purchasing decisions among French and Polish students, who expressed a willingness to shift behavior if sustainability claims were credible.

Knowledge gaps are a frequent issue. Nordin and Selke (2010) highlighted discrepancies between consumer attitudes and behaviors regarding sustainable packaging. Moreover, consumers tend to focus more on end-of-life attributes such as recyclability, while often neglecting production and material sourcing phases, transport, and retail use (Boesen et al., 2019; Herbes et al., 2018, 2020; Steenis et al., 2017).

Finally, sustainable packaging is acknowledged not only for reducing environmental impact but also for decreasing food waste and improving transport efficiency (Lindh et al., 2016b). However, the general misalignment between consumer perceptions and actual environmental impacts remains a critical challenge for both researchers and marketers.

3.6 Holistic Approaches

Several studies approach eco-friendly packaging from a broad perspective. Together, these studies demonstrate that a holistic understanding of eco-friendly packaging must consider both the tangible material aspects and the communicative, symbolic cues that impact consumers' responses.

Steenis et al. (2017) found that consumers' perceptions of packaging sustainability are influenced not only by the material used but also by graphical elements that might not correspond to actual environmental impact. Similarly, Herbes et al. (2020) highlighted the role of labeling as one of the first cues consumers associate with eco-friendliness, but also materials, amount, and color of the packaging were considered, while noting that social cues, such as peer communication, tend to have a lower perceived importance. Scott and Vigar-Ellis (2014) reported that consumers often rely on logos, labels, materials, and earth-tone colors (e.g., green, brown, cream) when evaluating the environmental credentials of packaging. However, uncertainty persists among some consumers regarding how to accurately recognize sustainable packaging. Zeng and Durif (2020) developed a conceptual framework exploring how eco-design features can contribute to reducing food waste. Their findings emphasize the relevance of packaging elements such as ease of closure, downsizing, and multi-packs, which support better food preservation. Verbal information, such as storage guidance and date labeling, also plays a role in communicating environmental benefits and promoting waste avoidance (Zeng et al., 2021).

Smith and Brower (2012), in a longitudinal study, identified the recycling symbol as the most powerful tool to communicate product sustainability, with product labeling following closely behind. Jerzyk (2016) revealed that consumers expected eco-friendly packaging to include messages about recyclability, material use, health, and safety, as well as minimal use of resources during production. Research by Arboretti and Bordignon (2016) showed that packaging material and shape, followed by biodegradability, re-closability, and shelf life, were highly valued attributes in the context of food products. Finally, Tran Dinh et al. (2022) proposed and validated a comprehensive six-dimensional scale for measuring eco-designed retail packaging, which includes functional attributes, aesthetic qualities, eco-material use, eco-information communication, eco-production processes, and innovation.

3.7 Analytical Approaches

A stream of research has focused on analyzing the effects of specific packaging cues and attributes on consumer responses. To classify and systematize sustainable packaging attributes from an analytical perspective, thus clarifying how packaging should be designed to be perceived as eco-friendly, it is first necessary to consider existing categorizations in the literature.

Magnier and Crié (2015) proposed a consumer-led taxonomy of eco-friendly packaging cues, highlighting a dual nature of ecological cues related to both product and packaging. They identified three primary categories:

(a) structural cues, referring to the physical aspects of packaging such as the reduction of packaging structure (e.g., elimination of overpackaging, packaging size and shape), materials (e.g., recycled, recyclable, renewable sources), and reusability;
(b) graphical cues, including visual elements such as colors, images, logos, and photographs;
(c) informational cues, encompassing environmental labeling, licensing agreements, general environmental claims, and scientific attributes.

Similarly, Herbes et al. (2020) recognized that cues could take different forms, either extrinsic (e.g., eco-labels) or intrinsic (e.g., materials), and identified four categories:

(a) structural cues, related to material type, size, and shape;
(b) visual cues, involving elements like colors, eco-labels, images, and photographs;
(c) informational cues, including numerical or verbal information about environmental impact;
(d) sensory cues, concerning tactile perceptions of the packaging.

This section follows the classifications of Magnier and Crié (2015) and Herbes et al. (2020), also reported in Branca et al. (2024).

3.7.1 Structural Cues

Structural cues refer to aspects such as the material composition and the size or shape of the packaging.

Regarding packaging material, numerous studies highlight a misalignment between consumers' perceptions and the actual environmental impact assessed through life cycle analysis (LCA). Boesen et al. (2019) investigated consumers' understanding of sustainable packaging across several product categories (e.g., soft drinks, beer, milk, olive oil, skinned tomatoes). The findings reveal that consumers primarily focus on material type and disposal attributes, overlooking production and transportation impacts. Materials like glass and bio-based plastics were perceived as the most eco-friendly options, whereas laminated cartons and plastics, despite sometimes being environmentally preferable, were seen less favorably. Similarly, Herbes et al. (2018) pointed out discrepancies between perceived and actual sustainability. The evaluations heavily rely on end-of-life attributes like recyclability, reusability and biodegradability rather than considering the entire life cycle. Steenis et al. (2017) further confirmed these misconceptions. In their study comparing seven packaging types for tomato soup, glass and bioplastics were perceived as more sustainable, even though actual LCA data did not always support these beliefs, followed by the liquid carton, plastic pouch, mixed pouch, dry carton sachet and can. Consistent findings emerge in the wine industry, where glass bottles remain the preferred format despite their significant environmental footprint (Ferrara et al., 2020). Furthermore, De Feo et al. (2022) found that even environmentally conscious consumers rank glass bottles as more sustainable than aluminum cans or plastic bottles, the latter being the least favored option. Other studies reinforce the consumer bias in favor of paper and biodegradable materials (e.g., Lindh et al., 2016a; Nguyen et al., 2020;), although recent research suggests a growing acceptance of recycled plastics when consumers recognize their environmental benefits (Ruokamo et al., 2022). However, shifts in consumer sentiment have been noted. Kitz et al. (2022) reported that after the COVID-19 pandemic, consumers showed a modest decline in motivation to reduce plastic usage, coupled with a decrease in support for stricter regulations or bans on single-use plastics. This suggests that health and safety concerns may temporarily outweigh environmental priorities in shaping packaging preferences.

Size and shape also play a critical role in sustainability perceptions. Overpackaging, namely the outer packaging designed to surround the product without any grouping of primary units, is increasingly criticized. Consumers associate excessive product packaging with greenwashing and unnecessary waste (Qayyum et al., 2022). Studies found that poor packaging design contributes significantly to food waste; consumers prefer packaging that is easy to empty, reclose and dose (Williams et al., 2012, 2020). Overpackaging elimination, however, yields mixed results. While it can signal eco-friendliness, it may also reduce perceptions of quality, protection, and purchase intentions (Monnot et al., 2015, 2019). Elgaaïed-Gambier (2016) showed that although consumers criticize overpackaging, they sometimes associate it with better product quality and brand prestige. Research on e-commerce packaging reveals some cultural variations. In China, as an example, consumers prioritize innovations like improved recycling systems and larger-scale packaging solutions over simply adopting green materials (Lu et al., 2020), indicating that technological improvements are valued over material changes. Finally, the purchase and consumption of packaging-free products seems to become a new sustainable consumption trend (Louis et al., 2021).

3.7.2 *Visual Cues*

Visual elements such as eco-labels, logos, brands, colors, images, and pictures play a relevant role in signaling sustainability. Borin et al. (2011) showed that labels conveying positive environmental messages enhance perceived product quality, value, and purchase intention, compared to negative labels. However, visual cues do not always produce uniform effects. Wood et al. (2018) found that mainstream brands promoting eco-friendliness through packaging visuals may experience diminished consumer efficacy evaluations and choice shares when compared to niche green brands. Recent evidence from Herédia-Colaço (2023) further suggests that promoting sustainable packaging is more effective when coming from less familiar brands rather than highly familiar ones. The isolated use of environmental cues also shows potential drawbacks. Pancer et al. (2017) found that presenting eco-labels without complementary green coloring, or vice versa, tends to decrease perceived product efficacy and purchase intentions. However, while green is typically associated with environmentalism and CSR, it is not always the most effective or credible option. Barchiesi et al. (2018) tested different packaging colors, green, blue, and white, across four product categories. Blue was found to be the most attractive and the most effective at conveying CSR messages clearly and credibly and in generating willingness to pay a premium price. White improved message clarity and credibility for deodorant and bottled water. The communicative power of green packaging may also be moderated by gender perceptions. Felix et al. (2021) examined the role of the color green in eco-friendly product design, finding that green was perceived as less masculine, which could influence product evaluations depending on gender expectations. Similarly, Sekki et al. (2023) called for greater attention to color as a tool for influencing sustainability perceptions, especially as consumers become more visually literate and skeptical. Finally, Marozzo et al. (2020), through a series of experiments involving packaging, defined au naturel colors, a novel color family that includes hues of beige, e.g., cream, sandy beiges, and mellow browns, and it is considered natural, organic, and earthy.

In terms of perceived product healthiness and sustainability, Cho and Baskin (2018) observed that products are evaluated more favorably when there is a strong perceived match between healthiness and sustainability levels. Nevertheless, they also noted that skepticism toward sustainability claims can inhibit the positive effects of eco-labels.

3.7.3 Information on Environmental Impact and Claims

Some studies focus specifically on the role of informational content, such as general environmental assertions, numerical or verbal claims, licensing agreements, and scientific or pedagogical attributes, in shaping consumers' evaluations of eco-friendly packaging.

Wei et al. (2018) investigated the influence of on-package CSR claims on consumer inferences and behavioral intentions. Their findings showed that CSR claims affect perceived healthiness, attitudes toward the company, purchase intention, and willingness to pay a premium price. In their study, different CSR domains were manipulated, namely eco-friendly packaging, food manufacturing practices, and employee welfare, across two types of food products (essential vs. indulgent). Eco-friendly packaging claims were primarily associated with credibility traits. Notably, among the three domains, eco-friendly packaging claims generated the lowest willingness to pay a premium.

At the industry level, Cousté et al. (2012) analyzed 18.000 consumer-packaged goods from 81 US firms, finding that environmental claims, such as recyclable or recycled materials, reduced packaging, refillable or reusable formats, and biodegradability, were the least frequently used among packaging claims. Moreover, environmental claims showed no significant impact on firm value. Within food and beverage products, recyclable packaging emerged as the most common environmental assertion.

Regarding the style of communication, Aagerup et al. (2019) examined the effects of rational versus emotional green packaging claims on purchase intention. Results indicated that green claims, whether emotional or rational, were preferred over neutral claims. However, emotional green claims had a stronger positive effect than rational ones. Furthermore, consumers' environmental commitment, cognitive processing ability, and distraction level moderated the impact of these claims.

3.7.4 Sensory Cues

Sensory cues relate to the tactile and material properties of packaging as perceived by consumers, influencing their evaluation of sustainability. Karana (2012) conducted an empirical study to explore how material characteristics contribute to perceptions of naturalness and quality. Findings indicated that materials perceived as opaque, non-reflective, warm, rough, and heavy were more associated with naturalness and environmental friendliness. Additional features reinforcing this perception included visible grains and fibers, irregular patterns, surface degradation, minimal processing, or traditional processing methods where the original material remains recognizable. Building on this, Karana and Nijkamp (2014) further investigated the impact of fibrousness, reflectiveness, and roughness on material appraisals. Their results confirmed that tactile sensations such as texture and surface properties play a key role in consumers' environmental perceptions of packaging. Extending these findings, Branca et al. (2023) demonstrated that rough, opaque packaging surfaces are perceived as more sustainable compared to smooth, reflective ones. Chen (2021) offered additional insights by examining the effects of matte versus glossy packaging. Matte surfaces, characterized by a rougher and softer touch and more diffused light reflections, elicited stronger consumer evaluations and higher purchase intentions than glossy surfaces, which are smooth, hard, and have single-angle light reflections. Matte packaging elicits stronger consumer evaluation and purchase intention than glossy packaging.

3.7.5 Cues Combinations

Some studies have investigated how different types of cues, such as claims, labels, materials, colors, and images, interact to influence consumer perceptions of eco-friendly packaging.

Magnier and Schoormans (2015) examined how visual appearance and verbal claims jointly affect consumer responses. Their findings showed that an eco-friendly visual appearance alone positively influenced consumers with high environmental concerns, even in the absence of explicit sustainability claims. Conversely, consumers with low environmental concerns were more sensitive to inconsistencies: when sustainability claims appeared on conventional-looking packaging, they reacted negatively. This suggests that perceived incongruence can undermine trust, particularly among less environmentally involved consumers, and that greenwashing practices could result in lower perceived ethicality and reduced purchase intentions. More recent research by Zeng et al. (2021) found that consumers respond more to visual improvements in packaging than to verbal sustainability claims.

Steenis et al. (2018) explored consumer reactions to circular versus linear design strategies, manipulating information about packaging redesign combined with icons to indicate whether the approach was circular (e.g., use of biodegradable materials) or linear (e.g., lightened material). Consumers preferred packaging redesigned with a single sustainable strategy over combinations of multiple strategies, perceiving it as marginally more sustainable. Additional sustainable features did not significantly boost purchase intention or willingness to pay a premium price.

Color also plays an important role in cue interpretation. Seo and Scammon (2017) showed that packaging colors enhance aesthetic appeal and information processing fluency. For instance, green can facilitate fluency when paired with affirmative environmental claims. However, green coloring on packaging can also mislead consumers, creating a false perception of environmental superiority even for non-sustainable brands.

The interaction between environmental labels and claims also affects consumer perceptions. Ertz et al. (2017) found that pairing self-declared claims with certified environmental labels increases consumers' perception of information credibility and perceived product quality. Donato et al. (2021) demonstrated that sustainable packaging can enhance perceived food satiation because it triggers higher perceived quality, while Donato and D'Aniello (2022) showed that combining eco-labels with environmental claims can boost food safety perceptions.

Environmental advertising strategies also interact with sustainability labels. Cho (2015) showed that when advertisements stress personal responsibility for the environment, consumers are more likely to view sustainability claims favorably and pay a premium price. If the advertisement instead highlights the company's environmental impact without a sustainability claim, highly environmentally involved consumers respond more positively toward the firm, whereas low-involvement consumers prefer messages that emphasize personal consumption consequences.

Gosselt et al. (2019) compared the effects of internal claims (e.g., statements about using recycled materials) and external third-party CSR labels. They found that external labels had a stronger positive effect on consumer attitudes toward the company, while internal claims alone were not significant. Combining claims and labels only marginally influenced purchase intentions. Additionally, positive external CSR labels elicited more favorable reactions than negative ones.

Moreover, Spack et al. (2012) found that the presence of green visual cues on packaging positively influenced purchase intention. While the strength of the accompanying environmental argument affected perceived credibility and attitudes toward product greenness, both strong and weak arguments were similarly effective at increasing purchasing intention. Importantly, a green image alone also boosted purchase intention, even without a strong argument.

Finally, Binninger (2017) investigated how different combinations of visual and textual cues shape perceptions of food naturalness and sustainability. By integrating colors, images, logos, labels, and claims into emotional, functional, and mixed packaging designs, the study found that mixed packaging (combining emotional and functional elements) was perceived as the most natural. Furthermore, subjective responses like attractiveness and purchase intent were more influenced by perceived health benefits, while objective product evaluations such as credibility and quality were more closely linked to environmental naturalness.

3.8 Consumers' Responses to Sustainable Packaging

To conclude, while the previous section focused on the effects of individual and combined cues, it is equally important to explore how consumers respond more generally to sustainable packaging. Some studies offer a broader perspective on attitudes and behaviors toward eco-friendly packaging. Five main themes emerge, providing a solid understanding of how sustainable packaging influences consumer decision-making.

First, eco-friendly packaging seems increasingly valued and preferred. For dairy products, Baruk and Iwanicka (2016) showed that ecology, intended as environmental performance, was among the most important packaging attributes, particularly for consumers highly concerned with environmental issues. From a broader functionality perspective, Dopico-Parada et al., (2021) identified sustainability as one of the core packaging attributes valued by consumers. Mancini et al. (2017) confirmed that recyclable packaging is one of six sustainable factors influencing consumption behavior. However, educational level moderates sensitivity: highly educated consumers are more critical of overpackaging, while those with lower education levels show less concern. Zeng (2022) noted that financial, functional, and social barriers can hinder the adoption of eco-designed packaging, although Granato et al. (2022) demonstrated that eco-packaging can simultaneously enhance perceptions of convenience, aesthetic quality, and product preservation, helping to mitigate potential disadvantages.

Second, sustainable packaging can influence attitudes and purchase intentions (Lisboa et al., 2022), but literature presents some mixed results. Prakash and Pathak (2017) highlighted that personal norms, willingness to pay, environmental concerns, and positive attitudes toward eco-packaging predict purchase intention. Among ethical product attributes, recyclable packaging had the greatest influence on purchasing decisions but generated the least added value, according to Mai (2014). Steenis et al. (2017) observed that although eco-friendliness is a salient association for consumers, it was only moderately important in forming product attitudes. Rees et al. (2019) found a discrepancy between high recognition of sustainability cues and actual purchasing behavior, suggesting that recognition does not necessarily translate into action. Trivedi et al. (2018) further emphasized that environmental attitudes and positive perceptions of eco-friendly packaging jointly shape green purchase intentions.

Third, willingness to pay (WTP) for sustainable packaging is mixed. Singh and Pandey (2018) identified six drivers of WTP for eco-friendly packaging: epistemic, functional, economic, symbolic, altruistic, and biospheric values. Nevertheless, Aagerup et al. (2019) found that eco-friendly packaging claims produced relatively low WTP for premium pricing. Ertz et al. (2017) similarly reported no significant WTP increase associated with the presence of environmental claims and labels. Wei et al. (2018) confirmed that eco-friendly packaging elicited only a limited WTP more. On a more positive note, Barber (2010) indicated that collectivism and pro-environmental attitudes predicted WTP for green wine packaging. Kitz et al. (2022) also found greater WTP for biodegradable alternatives after the pandemic, signaling evolving consumer priorities.

Fourth, packaging design affects product perceptions. Steenis et al. (2017) demonstrated that altering packaging materials influenced perceptions of sustainability, quality, and taste. Similarly, Binninger (2017) noted that sustainability associations can overlap with perceptions of naturalness and healthiness. Magnier et al. (2016) found that sustainable packaging boosts perceived food quality, although this effect is moderated by the overall sustainability of the product itself. Perceived naturalness mediated the interaction between product and packaging sustainability in shaping quality perceptions. Skard et al. (2020) highlighted a sustainability liability effect in functional products (like drain openers) where eco-packaging reduced perceived product strength, contrasting with a sustainability asset effect observed for gentle-dependent products (like body lotion).

Fifth, personal and marketing stimuli influence sustainable shopping behavior. Prakash et al. (2019) found that altruistic and egoistic values both positively influence eco-packaging adoption, although altruistic values exert a stronger effect. Shimul and Cheah (2023) highlighted that environmental responsibility and knowledge influence the intention to adopt eco-packaging through the mediating role of attitude. Emotions also play a critical role: Koenig-Lewis et al. (2014) found that emotional responses are stronger drivers of sustainable purchase behavior than rational evaluations. Both positive and negative emotions impact purchase intentions, but positive emotions have a greater influence when associated with eco-friendly packaging. Scott and Vigar-Ellis (2014) emphasized the role of environmental knowledge in directly and indirectly shaping environmentally friendly behaviors. Finally, attractiveness is another key element: according to Magnier and Schoormans (2015), attractive packaging design enhances consumer responses, and perceived brand ethicality mediates the relationship between sustainability cues, environmental concern, and purchase intention.

3.9 Conclusions and Implications

The literature review on sustainable packaging and consumer behavior offers several insights and implications for both researchers and practitioners.

This chapter offers a comprehensive contribution to the study of sustainable packaging from a consumer behavior perspective by addressing several limitations in previous reviews. While earlier literature has often framed packaging within broad (e.g., Afif et al., 2022; Akturan et al., 2025; Baskoro et al., 2024; Lau & Wong, 2024) or sector-specific sustainability discussions (e.g., Bangsa & Schlegelmilch, 2020; Baskoro et al., 2024; Brennan et al., 2021), this contribution distinguishes itself by providing a consumer-centered categorization of sustainability-related packaging cues. Building on Branca et al. (2024), the chapter organizes the fragmented body of knowledge into an integrated analytical framework that enhances the conceptual clarity on how packaging attributes and cues influence consumer responses.

The review highlights that consumers' knowledge and understanding of eco-friendly packaging remains partial and often inconsistent. Consumers may recognize sustainability-related cues yet misinterpret their actual environmental value. Several motivations and barriers to adopting or opting for more sustainable packaging solutions emerged, calling for future research that sheds more light on the fragmented and evolving consumers' responses.

Holistic approaches have been essential to framing eco-friendly packaging as a perceptual and evaluative construct (e.g., Herbes et al., 2020; Steenis et al., 2017). These studies examine how consumers interpret packaging as a whole and its global appearance. However, they generally do not disaggregate the effects of specific design elements, leaving open questions about the individual role of each specific cue and attribute.

The analytical approach presented here advances the field by distinguishing the main categories of sustainability-related cues, such as structural cues, visual cues, information on environmental impacts and claims, sensory cues, and the combination of some of them. This taxonomy, grounded in prior classifications (e.g., Branca et al., 2024; Herbes et al., 2020; Magnier & Crié, 2015), allows a more granular understanding of how different packaging attributes elicit distinct consumer responses. Structural cues (e.g., material, size, reusability) and informational cues (e.g., claims, labels) emerged as particularly relevant in previous literature, while little attention has been given to sensory cues.

Finally, the analysis of consumer attitudes and behaviors toward sustainable packaging highlights a complex set of cognitive, emotional, and contextual factors. While sustainability positively influences consumers' responses, it does not always translate into willingness to pay a premium price or change purchase behavior, for example when consumers face competing goals or limited information.

Despite the growing attention to sustainable packaging in consumer research, most studies reviewed in this chapter have been conducted in physical or in-store contexts, with limited exploration of how packaging is perceived and evaluated in digital environments. Yet, as shopping behavior continues to shift toward online, augmented, and

VR marketplaces (Akturan et al., 2025), understanding how packaging communicates sustainability in these immersive settings becomes increasingly relevant. The findings synthesized in this chapter create a foundation for leveraging immersive technologies to address sustainability challenges in packaging. Virtual prototyping enables companies to experiment with design cues (structural, haptic, and visual) while simultaneously measuring consumers' attitudes and intentions. By embedding sustainability evaluation into immersive consumer testing, marketers can make evidence-based decisions earlier in the innovation cycle, reducing the environmental footprint of physical prototyping and supporting regulatory compliance. Thus, this chapter informs the experimental design presented in the following ones, where VR becomes a bridge between sustainable design principles and consumer insights, and provides new insights into the dynamics of consumer–packaging interaction beyond traditional contexts.

References

Aagerup, U., Frank, A. S., & Hultqvist, E. (2019). The persuasive effects of emotional green packaging claims. *British Food Journal, 121*(12), 3233–3246. https://doi.org/10.1108/BFJ-08-2019-0652

Aday, M. S., & Yener, U. (2014). Understanding the buying behaviour of young consumers regarding packaging attributes and labels. *International Journal of Consumer Studies, 38*(4), 385–393. https://doi.org/10.1111/ijcs.12105

Afif, K., Rebolledo, C., & Roy, J. (2022). Drivers, barriers and performance outcomes of sustainable packaging: A systematic literature review. *British Food Journal, 124*(3), 915–935. https://doi.org/10.1108/BFJ-02-2021-0150

Akturan, U., Kuter, D., & Gökkut, B. S. (2025). Mirror, mirror on the wall, who is the most convincing of them all? A systematic literature review on packaging. *Journal of Business Research, 193*, Article 115355. https://doi.org/10.1016/j.jbusres.2025.115355

Arboretti, R., & Bordignon, P. (2016). Consumer preferences in food packaging: CUB models and conjoint analysis. *British Food Journal, 118*(3), 527–540. https://doi.org/10.1108/BFJ-04-2015-0146

Bangsa, A., & Schlegelmilch, B. B. (2020). Linking sustainable product attributes and consumer decision-making: Insights from a systematic review. *Journal of Cleaner Production, 245*, Article 118902. https://doi.org/10.1016/j.jclepro.2019.118902

Barber, N. (2010). "Green" wine packaging. Targeting environmental consumers. *International Journal of Wine Business Research, 22(4)*, 423–444. https://doi.org/10.1108/17511061011092447.

Barchiesi, M. A., Castellan, S., & Costa, R. (2018). In the eye of the beholder: Communicating CSR through color in packaging design. *Journal of Marketing Communications, 24*(7), 720–733. https://doi.org/10.1080/13527266.2016.1224771

Baruk, A. I., & Iwanicka, A. (2016). The effect of age, gender and level of education on the consumer's expectations towards dairy product packaging. *British Food Journal, 118*(1), 100–118. https://doi.org/10.1108/BFJ-07-2015-0248

Baskoro, M. L., Tjahjono, B., Beltran, M., Bogush, A., & Wang, Y. (2024). The imperative of communication signals in boosting business strategies of the bioplastic packaging industry. *Business Strategy and the Environment, 33*(2), 307–334. https://doi.org/10.1002/bse.3490

Binninger, A. S. (2017). Perception of naturalness of food packaging and its role in consumer product evaluation. *Journal of Food Products Marketing, 23*(3), 251–266. https://doi.org/10.1080/10454446.2014.885868

Boesen, S., Bey, N., & Niero, M. (2019). Environmental sustainability of liquid food packaging. Is there a gap between Danish consumers' perception and learnings from life cycle assessment? *Journal of Cleaner Production, 210*, 1193–1206. https://doi.org/10.1016/j.jclepro.2018.11.055

Boks, C., & Stevels, A., (2007). Essential perspectives for design for environment. Experiences from the electronics industry. *International Journal of Production Research, 45(18–19)*, 4021–4039. https://doi.org/10.1080/00207540701439909

Borin, N., Cerf, D. C., & Krishnan, R. (2011). Consumer effects of environmental impact in product labelling. *Journal of Consumer Marketing, 28*(1), 76–86. https://doi.org/10.1108/07363761111101976

Branca, G., Resciniti, R., & Babin, B. J. (2024). Sustainable packaging design and the consumer perspective: A systematic literature review. *Italian Journal of Marketing*, 77–111. https://doi.org/10.1007/s43039-023-00084-1

Branca, G., Resciniti, R., & Loureiro, S. M. C. (2023). Virtual is so real! Consumers' evaluation of product packaging in virtual reality. *Psychology & Marketing, 40*, 596–609. https://doi.org/10.1002/mar.21743

Brennan, L., Langley, S., Verghese, K., Lockrey, S., Ryder, M., Francis, C., Phan-Le, N. T., & Hill, A. (2021). The role of packaging in fighting food waste: A systematised review of consumer perceptions of packaging. *Journal of Cleaner Production, 281*, Article 125276. https://doi.org/10.1016/j.jclepro.2020.125276

Briand Decré, G., & Cloonan, C. (2019). A touch of gloss: Haptic perception of packaging and consumers' reactions. *Journal of Product & Brand Management, 28*(1), 117–132. https://doi.org/10.1108/JPBM-05-2017-1472

Canto Primo, M., Gil-Saura, I., & Frasquet-Deltoro, M. (2021). The role of marketing and product design in driving firm's performance. *Journal of Product & Brand Management, 30*(2), 231–243. https://doi.org/10.1108/JPBM-07-2019-2477

Chandon, P. (2013). How package design and packaged-based marketing claims lead to overeating. *Applied Economic Perspectives and Policy, 35*(1), 7–31. https://doi.org/10.1093/aepp/pps028

Chen, Y. S. A. (2021). Does outward appearance appeal to the inward mind? The impact of packaging finishes on brand impressions and the subsequent behavior of consumer. *Journal of Product & Brand Management, 30*(5), 768–778. https://doi.org/10.1108/JPBM-07-2019-2466

Cho, Y. N. (2015). Different shades of green consciousness: The interplay of sustainability labeling and environmental impact on product evaluations. *Journal of Business Ethics, 128*, 73–82. https://doi.org/10.1007/s10551-014-2080-4

Cho, Y. N., & Baskin, E. (2018). It's a match when green meets healthy in sustainability labelling. *Journal of Business Research, 86*, 119–129. https://doi.org/10.1016/j.jbusres.2018.01.050

Chrysochou, P., & Festila, A. (2019). A content analysis of organic product package designs. *Journal of Consumer Marketing, 36*(4), 441–448. https://doi.org/10.1108/JCM-06-2018-2720

Coelho do Vale, R., & Verga Matos, P. (2015). The impact of copycat packaging strategies on the adoption of private labels. *Journal of Product & Brand Management, 24*(6), 646–659. https://doi.org/10.1108/JPBM-03-2015-0846

Cousté, N. L., Martos-Partal, M., & Martinez-Ros, E. (2012). The Power of a Package Product Claims Drive Purchase Decisions. *Journal of Advertising Research, 52*(3), 364–375. https://doi.org/10.2501/JAR-52-3-364-375

De Feo, G., Ferrara, C., & Francesca Minichini, F. (2022). Comparison between the perceived and actual environmental sustainability of beverage packagings in glass, plastic, and aluminium. *Journal of Cleaner Production, 333*, Article 130158. https://doi.org/10.1016/j.jclepro.2021.130158

Donato, C., Barone, A. M., & Romani, S. (2021). The satiating power of sustainability: The effect of package sustainability on perceived satiation of healthy food. *British Food Journal, 123*(13), 162–177. https://doi.org/10.1108/BFJ-12-2020-1094

Donato, C., & D'Aniello, A. (2022). Tell me more and make me feel proud: The role of eco-labels and informational cues on consumers' food perceptions. *British Food Journal, 124*(4), 1365–1382. https://doi.org/10.1108/BFJ-04-2021-0416

Dopico-Parada, A., López-Miguens, M., & Álvarez-González, P. (2021). Building value with packaging: Development and validation of a measurement scale. *Journal of Retailing and Consumer Services, 63,* Article 102685. https://doi.org/10.1016/j.jretconser.2021.102685

Du, S., Bhattacharya, C. B., & Sen, S. (2010). Maximizing business returns to corporate social responsibility (CSR): The role of CSR communication. *International Journal of Management Reviews, 12*(1), 8–19. https://doi.org/10.1111/j.1468-2370.2009.00276.x

Eberhart, A. K., & Naderer, G. (2017). Quantitative and qualitative insights into consumers' sustainable purchasing behaviour: A segmentation approach based on motives and heuristic cues. *Journal of Marketing Management, 33*(13–14), 1149–1169. https://doi.org/10.1080/0267257X.2017.1371204

Elgaaïed-Gambier, L. (2016). Who buys overpackaged grocery products and why? Understanding consumers' reactions to overpackaging in the food sector. *Journal of Business Ethics, 135,* 683–698. https://doi.org/10.1007/s10551-014-2491-2

Ertz, M., François, J., & Durif, F. (2017). How consumers react to environmental information. An experimental study. *Journal of International Consumer Marketing, 29(3),* 162–178. https://doi.org/10.1080/08961530.2016.1273813.

Fajardo, T. M., & Townsend, C. (2016). Where you say it matters: Why packages are a more believable source of product claims than advertisements. *Journal of Consumer Psychology, 26*(3), 426–434. https://doi.org/10.1016/j.jcps.2015.11.002

Felix, R., González, E. M., Castaño, R., Carrete, L., & Gretz, R. T. (2021). When the green in green packaging backfires: Gender effects and perceived masculinity of environmentally friendly products. *International Journal of Consumer Studies, 00,* 1–19. https://doi.org/10.1111/ijcs.12738

Ferrara, C., Zigarelli, V., & De Feo, G. (2020). Attitudes of a sample of consumers towards more sustainable wine packaging alternatives. *Journal of Cleaner Production, 271,* Article 122581. https://doi.org/10.1016/j.jclepro.2020.122581

Festila, A., & Chrysochou, P. (2018). Implicit communication of food product healthfulness through package design: A content analysis. *Journal of Consumer Behavior, 17,* 461–476. https://doi.org/10.1002/cb.1732

Gofman, A., Moskowitz, H. R., & Mets, T. (2010). Accelerating structured consumer-driven package design. *Journal of Consumer Marketing, 27*(2), 157–168. https://doi.org/10.1108/07363761011027259

Gosselt, J. F., van Rompay, T., & Haske, L. (2019). Won't get fooled again: The effects of internal and external CSR ECO-Labeling. *Journal of Business Ethics, 155,* 413–424. https://doi.org/10.1007/s10551-017-3512-8

Granato, G., Fischer, A. H. R., & van Trijp, H. C. M. (2022). The price of sustainability: How consumers trade-off conventional packaging benefits against sustainability. *Journal of Cleaner Production, 365,* Article 132739. https://doi.org/10.1016/j.jclepro.2022.132739

Herbes, C., Beuthner, C., & Ramme, I. (2018). Consumer attitudes towards biobased packaging. A cross-cultural comparative study. *Journal of Cleaner Production, 194(1),* 203–218. https://doi.org/10.1016/j.jclepro.2018.05.106.

Herbes, C., Beuthner, C., & Ramme, I. (2020). How green is your packaging—A comparative international study of cues consumers use to recognize environmentally friendly packaging. *International Journal of Consumer Studies, 44*(3), 258–271. https://doi.org/10.1111/ijcs.12560

Herédia-Colaço, V. (2023). Pro-environmental messages have more effect when they come from less familiar brands. *Journal of Product & Brand Management, 32*(3), 436–453. https://doi.org/10.1108/JPBM-12-2021-3782

Holmes, G. R., & Paswan, A. (2012). Consumer reaction to new package design. *Journal of Product & Brand Management, 21*(2), 109–116. https://doi.org/10.1108/10610421211215553

Hoornweg, D., & Bhada-Tata, P. (2012). *What a Waste: A Global Review of Solid Waste Management*. Urban development series (Knowledge papers no. 15). World Bank, https://openknowledge.worldbank.org/handle/10986/17388

Hwang, J., & Kim, S. (2022). The effects of packaging design of private brands on consumers' responses. *Psychology & Marketing, 39*, 777–796. https://doi.org/10.1002/mar.21620

Jerzyk, E. (2016). Design and communication of ecological content on sustainable packaging in young consumers' opinions. *Journal of Food Products Marketing, 22*(6), 707–716. https://doi.org/10.1080/10454446.2015.1121435

Karana, E. (2012). Characterization of 'natural' and 'high-quality' materials to improve perception of bio-plastics. *Journal of Cleaner Production, 37*, 316–325. https://doi.org/10.1016/j.jclepro.2012.07.034

Karana, E., & Nijkamp, N. (2014). Fiberness, reflectiveness and roughness in the characterization of natural and high quality materials. *Journal of Cleaner Production, 68*, 252–260. https://doi.org/10.1016/j.jclepro.2014.01.001

Kemper, J. A., & Ballantine, P. W. (2019). What do we mean by sustainability marketing? *Journal of Marketing Management, 35*(3–4), 277–309. https://doi.org/10.1080/0267257X.2019.1573845

Ketelsen, M., Janssen, M., & Hamm, U. (2020). Consumers' response to environmentally-friendly food packaging - A systematic review. *Journal of Cleaner Production, 254*, Article 120123. https://doi.org/10.1016/j.jclepro.2020.120123

Kitz, R., Walker, T., Charlebois, S., & Music, J. (2022). Food packaging during the COVID-19 pandemic: Consumer perceptions. *International Journal of Consumer Studies, 46*, 434–448. https://doi.org/10.1111/ijcs.12691

Koenig-Lewis, N., Palmer, A., Dermody, J., & Urbye, A. (2014). Consumers' evaluations of ecological packaging. Rational and emotional approaches. *Journal of Environmental Psychology, 37*, 94–105. https://doi.org/10.1016/j.jenvp.2013.11.009

Ku, H.-H., & Chen, Y. (2023). Naming product colors with an individual's identity and product evaluation: Self-referencing as a mediator. *Journal of Product & Brand Management, 32*(6), 958–971. https://doi.org/10.1108/JPBM-12-2021-3791

Lau, C. C. I., & Wong, C. W. Y. (2024). Achieving sustainable development with sustainable packaging: A natural-resource-based view perspective. *Business Strategy and the Environment, 33*(5), 4766–4787. https://doi.org/10.1002/bse.3720

Liao, L. L., Corsi, A. M., Chrysochou, P., & Larry Lockshin, L. (2015). Emotional responses towards food packaging: A joint application of self-report and physiological measures of emotion. *Food Quality and Preference, 42*, 48–55. https://doi.org/10.1016/j.foodqual.2015.01.009

Lindh, H., Olsson, A., & Williams, H. (2016a). Consumer perceptions of food packaging: contributing to or counteracting environmentally sustainable development? *Packaging Technology and Science, 29(3–23)*. https://doi.org/10.1002/pts.2184

Lindh, H., Williams, H., Olsson, A., & Wikström, F. (2016b). Elucidating the indirect contributions of packaging to sustainable development. A terminology of packaging functions and features. *Packaging Technology and Science, 29(4–5)*, 225–246. https://doi.org/10.1002/pts.2197

Lisboa, A., Vitorino, L., & Antunes, R. (2022). Gen Zers' intention to purchase products with sustainable packaging: An alternative perspective to the attitude-behaviour gap. *Journal of Marketing Management, 38*(9–10), 967–992. https://doi.org/10.1080/0267257X.2022.2083214

Littel, S., & Orth, U. R. (2013). Effects of package visuals and haptics on brand evaluations. *European Journal of Marketing, 47*(1/2), 198–217. https://doi.org/10.1108/03090561311285510

Louis, D., Lombart, C., & Durif, F. (2021). Packaging-free products: A lever of proximity and loyalty between consumers and grocery stores. *Journal of Retailing and Consumer Services, 60*, Article 102499. https://doi.org/10.1016/j.jretconser.2021.102499

Lu, S., Yang, L., Liu, W., & Jia, L. (2020). User preference for electronic commerce overpackaging solutions: Implications for cleaner production. *Journal of Cleaner Production, 258*, Article 120936. https://doi.org/10.1016/j.jclepro.2020.120936

Mai, L. W. (2014). Consumers' willingness to pay for ethical attributes. *Marketing Intelligence & Planning, 32*(6), 706–721. https://doi.org/10.1108/MIP-08-2013-0139

Magnier, L., & Crié, D. (2015). Communicating packaging eco-friendliness: An exploration of consumers' perceptions of eco-designed packaging. *International Journal of Retail & Distribution Management, 43*(4/5), 350–366. https://doi.org/10.1108/IJRDM-04-2014-0048

Magnier, L., & Schoormans, J. (2015). Consumer reactions to sustainable packaging: The interplay of visual appearance, verbal claim and environmental concern. *Journal of Environmental Psychology, 44*, 53–62. https://doi.org/10.1016/j.jenvp.2015.09.005

Magnier, L., Schoormans, J., & Mugge, R. (2016). Judging a product by its cover. Packaging sustainability and perceptions of quality in food products. *Food Quality and Preference, 53*, 132–142. https://doi.org/10.1016/j.foodqual.2016.06.006

Mancini, P., Marchini, A., & Simeone, M. (2017). Which are the sustainable attributes affecting the real consumption behaviour? Consumer understanding and choices. *British Food Journal, 119*, 1839–1853. https://doi.org/10.1108/BFJ-11-2016-0574

Marozzo, V., Raimondo, M. A., Miceli, G. "Nino," & Scopelliti, I. (2020). Effects of au naturel packaging colors on willingness to pay for healthy food. *Psychology & Marketing, 37(7)*, 913–927. https://doi.org/10.1002/mar.21294

Molina-Besch, K. (2016). Prioritization guidelines for green food packaging development. *British Food Journal, 118*(10), 2512–2533. https://doi.org/10.1108/BFJ-12-2015-0462

Monnot, E., Parguel, B., & Reniou, F. (2015). Consumer responses to elimination of overpackaging on private label products. *International Journal of Retail & Distribution Management, 43*(4/5), 329–349. https://doi.org/10.1108/IJRDM-03-2014-0036

Monnot, E., Reniou, F., Parguel, B., & Elgaaïed-Gambier, L. (2019). Thinking outside the packaging box: Should brands consider store shelf context when eliminating overpackaging? *Journal of Business Ethics, 154*, 355–370. https://doi.org/10.1007/s10551-017-3439-0

Nordin, N., & Selke, S. (2010). Social Aspect of Sustainable Packaging. *Packaging Technology and Science, 23*(6), 317–326. https://doi.org/10.1002/pts.899

Nguyen, A. T., Parker, L., Brennan, L., & Lockrey, S. (2020). A consumer definition of eco-friendly packaging. *Journal of Cleaner Production, 252*, Article 119792. https://doi.org/10.1016/j.jclepro.2019.119792

Olson, J. C. (1978). *Inferential belief formation in the cue utilization process*. In Advances in Consumer Research Volume 05 (pp. 706–713). Association for Consumer Research. https://www.acrwebsite.org/volumes/9509/volumes/v05/NA-05

Orth, U. R., & De Marchi, R. (2007). Endurance of advertising evoked brand image beliefs in the face of product trial. *Journal of Food Products Marketing, 13*(1), 31–44. https://doi.org/10.1300/J038v13n01_03

Pancer, E., McShane, L., & Noseworthy, T. J. (2017). Isolated environmental cues and product efficacy penalties: The color green and eco-labels. *Journal of Business Ethics, 143*, 159–177. https://doi.org/10.1007/s10551-015-2764-4

Park, J., & Ma, Y. J. (2019). Number-location bias: Do consumers correctly process the number on the product package? *Journal of Product & Brand Management, 28*(1), 80–94. https://doi.org/10.1108/JPBM-12-2017-1711

Prakash, G., Choudhary, S., Kumar, A., Garza-Reyes, J. A., Khan, S. A. R., & Panda, T. K. (2019). Do altruistic and egoistic values influence consumers' attitudes and purchase intentions towards eco-friendly packaged products? An empirical investigation. *Journal of Retailing and Consumer Services, 50*, 163–169. https://doi.org/10.1016/j.jretconser.2019.05.011

Prakash, G., & Pathak, P. (2017). Intention to buy eco-friendly packaged products among young consumers of India. A study on developing nation. *Journal of Cleaner Production, 141*, 385–393. https://doi.org/10.1016/j.jclepro.2016.09.116

Qayyum, A., Jamil, R. A., & Sehar, A. (2022). Impact of green marketing, greenwashing and green confusion on green brand equity. *Spanish Journal of Marketing—ESIC, 27*(3), 286–305. https://doi.org/10.1108/SJME-03-2022-0032

Qiao, F., & Griffin, W. G. (2022). Brand imitation strategy, package design and consumer response: What does it take to make a difference? *Journal of Product & Brand Management, 31*(2), 177–188. https://doi.org/10.1108/JPBM-05-2019-2363

Rees, W., Tremma, O., & Manning, L. (2019). Sustainability cues on packaging: The influence of recognition on purchasing behaviour. *Journal of Cleaner Production, 235*, 841–853. https://doi.org/10.1016/j.jclepro.2019.06.217

Resciniti, R. (2020). 2020: A new Journal for a true Marketing. *Italian Journal of Marketing, 1–2*. https://doi.org/10.1007/s43039-020-00007-4

Ruokamo, E., Räisänen, M., & Kauppi, S. (2022). Consumer preferences for recycled plastics: Observations from a citizen survey. *Journal of Cleaner Production, 379*(2), Article 134720. https://doi.org/10.1016/j.jclepro.2022.134720

Scott, L., & Vigar-Ellis, D. (2014). Consumer understanding, perceptions and behaviours with regard to environmentally friendly packaging in a developing nation. *International Journal of Consumer Studies, 38*(6), 642–649. https://doi.org/10.1111/ijcs.12136

Sekki, S., Kauppinen-Räisänen, H., Kylkilahti, E., & Autio, M. (2023). Packaging journey from retail to home: How the meaning of sustainability for colour transforms. *International Journal of Retail & Distribution Management, 51*(13), 47–63. https://doi.org/10.1108/IJRDM-12-2021-0579

Seo, J., & Scammon, D. (2017). Do green packages lead to misperceptions? The influence of package colors on consumers' perceptions of brands with environmental claims. *Marketing Letters, 28*, 357–369. https://doi.org/10.1007/s11002-017-9420-y

Shimul, A. S., & Cheah, I. (2023). Consumers' preference for eco-friendly packaged products: Pride vs guilt appeal. *Marketing Intelligence & Planning, 41*(2), 186–198. https://doi.org/10.1108/MIP-05-2022-0197

Singh, G., & Pandey, N. (2018). The determinants of green packaging that influence buyers' willingness to pay a price premium. *Australasian Marketing Journal, 26*(3), 221–230. https://doi.org/10.1016/j.ausmj.2018.06.001

Skard, S., Jørgensen, S., & Pedersen, L. J. T. (2020). When is sustainability a liability, and when is it an asset? Quality inferences for core and peripheral attributes. *Journal of Business Ethics, 173*, 109–132. https://doi.org/10.1007/s10551-019-04415-1

Smith, K. T., & Brower, T. R. (2012). Longitudinal study of green marketing strategies that influence Millennials. *Journal of Strategic Marketing, 20*(6), 535–551. https://doi.org/10.1080/0965254X.2012.711345

Söderlund, M., Colliander, J., Karsberg, J., Liljedal, K. T., Modig, E., Rosengren, S., Sagfossen, S., Szugalski, S., & Åkestam, N. (2017). The allure of the bottle as a package: An assessment of perceived effort in a packaging context. *Journal of Product & Brand Management, 26*(1), 91–100. https://doi.org/10.1108/JPBM-12-2015-1065

Spack, J. A., Board, V. E., Crighton, L. M., Kostka, P. M., & Ivory, J. D. (2012). It's easy being green: The effects of argument and imagery on consumer responses to green product packaging. *Environmental Communication, 6*(4), 441–458. https://doi.org/10.1080/17524032.2012.706231

Steenis, N. D., van der Lans, I. A., van Herpen, E., & van Trijp, H. C. M. (2018). Effects of sustainable design strategies on consumer preferences for redesigned packaging. *Journal of Cleaner Production, 205*, 854–865. https://doi.org/10.1016/j.jclepro.2018.09.137

Steenis, N. D., van Herpen, E., van der Lans, I. A., Ligthart, T. N., & van Trijp, H. C. M. (2017). Consumer response to packaging design. The role of packaging materials and graphics in sustainability perceptions and product evaluations. *Journal of Cleaner Production, 162*, 286–298. https://doi.org/10.1016/j.jclepro.2017.06.036

Sustainable Packaging Alliance. (2007). *Defining sustainable packaging*. http://www.sustainablepack.org/research/subpage_PageID_10_id_7.html

Sustainable Packaging Coalition. (2011). *Definition of sustainable packaging*. https://sustainablepackaging.org/wp-content/uploads/2019/06/Definition-of-Sustainable-Packaging.pdf

Tran Dinh, M. T., Su, D. N., Tran, K. T., Luu, T. T., Duong, T. H., & Johnson, L. W. (2022). Ecodesigned retail packaging: The empirical conceptualization and measurement. *Journal of Cleaner Production, 379*(2), Article 134717. https://doi.org/10.1016/j.jclepro.2022.134717

Trivedi, R. H., Patel, J. D., & Acharya, N. (2018). Causality analysis of media influence on environmental attitude, intention and behaviors leading to green purchasing. *Journal of Cleaner Production, 196*, 11–22. https://doi.org/10.1016/j.jclepro.2018.06.024

Venter, K., van der Merwe, D., de Beer, H., Kempen, E., & Bosman, M. (2011). Consumers' perceptions of food packaging. An exploratory investigation in Potchefstroom, South Africa. *International Journal of Consumer Studies, 35(3)*, 273–281. https://doi.org/10.1111/j.1470-6431.2010.00936.x

Wei, W., Kim, G., Miao, L., Behnke, C., & Almanza, B. (2018). Consumer inferences of corporate social responsibility (CSR) claims on packaged foods. *Journal of Business Research, 83*, 186–201. https://doi.org/10.1016/j.jbusres.2017.10.046

Wikström, F., Verghese, K., Auras, R., Olsson, A., Williams, H., Wever, R., Grönman, K., Kvalvåg Pettersen, M., Møller, H., & Soukka, R. (2018). Packaging strategies that save food: A research agenda for 2030. *Journal of Industrial Ecology, 23*(3), 532–540. https://doi.org/10.1111/jiec.12769

Wilkinson, S. (2008). *Focus Groups*. In G. M. Breakwell (Ed.), *Doing Social Psychology Research*. Wiley-Blackwell.

Williams, H., Lindström, A., Trischler, J., Wikström, F., & Rowe, Z. (2020). Avoiding food becoming waste in households—The role of packaging in consumers' practices across different food categories. *Journal of Cleaner Production, 265*, Article 121775. https://doi.org/10.1016/j.jclepro.2020.121775

Williams, H., Wikström, F., Otterbring, T., Löfgren, M., & Gustafsson, A. (2012). Reasons for household food waste with special attention to packaging. *Journal of Cleaner Production, 24*, 141–148. https://doi.org/10.1016/j.jclepro.2011.11.044

Wood, S., Robinson, S., & Poor, M. (2018). The efficacy of green package cues for mainstream versus niche brands. How mainstream green brands can suffer at the shelf. *Journal of Advertising Research, 58(2)*, 165–176. https://doi.org/10.2501/JAR-2018-025

Zeng, T. (2022). Impacts of consumers' perceived risks in eco-design packaging on food wastage behaviors. *British Food Journal, 124*(8), 2512–2532. https://doi.org/10.1108/BFJ-05-2021-0603

Zeng, T., Deschênes, J., & Durif, F. (2020). Eco-design packaging: An epistemological analysis and transformative research agenda. *Journal of Cleaner Production, 276*, Article 123361. https://doi.org/10.1016/j.jclepro.2020.123361

Zeng, T., & Durif, F. (2020). The impact of eco-design packaging on food waste avoidance: A conceptual framework. *Journal of Promotion Management, 26*(5), 768–790. https://doi.org/10.1080/10496491.2020.1729320

Zeng, T., Durif, F., & Robinot, E. (2021). Can eco-design packaging reduce consumer food waste? An experimental study. *Technological Forecasting & Social Change,* 162, 120342. https://doi.org/10.1016/j.techfore.2020.120342

Chapter 4
Research Design and Methodology

4.1 Research Questions and Objectives

Recent research has begun comparing VR with other experimental conditions, although comparisons with PR remain limited and rarely address attitudes toward specific product attributes (Hilken et al., 2022). Most VR studies focus on holistic product evaluations or consumer behavior at the shelf or store level, rather than analytical assessments of product features. While existing literature generally finds that consumer behavior in VR aligns with that in PR, it remains unclear how consumers evaluate specific packaging cues, such as material, texture, or color, when presented in a virtual setting. To date, this area has received limited attention.

As highlighted by Akturan et al. (2025), most studies on packaging and consumer behavior have been conducted in physical retail environments, with scarce attention paid to online or immersive digital settings. Given the increasing relevance of VR in retail and product testing contexts, it becomes essential to explore how consumers perceive and respond to packaging cues in virtual environments.

This gap raises critical questions.

How do consumers evaluate packaged products in VR compared to PR?
Are there differences in consumer responses between these two conditions?

The central objective of this research is to explore potential differences in consumer evaluations of packaging when experienced in VR versus PR. To do so, the research focuses on three key types of packaging cues, structural, haptic, and visual, employing an FMCG, namely a milk pack, as the reference product. For each cue type, three packaging alternatives were developed (as detailed in Sect. 4.4):

(a) structural—glass bottle, baseline carton, plastic bottle;
(b) haptic—rough carton, baseline carton, smooth carton;
(c) visual—green carton, baseline carton, beige carton.

G. Branca, *Virtual Reality, Real Intentions*, International Series in Advanced Management Studies, https://doi.org/10.1007/978-3-032-10142-6_4

Because VR can accurately simulate visual aspects of PR, it is reasonable to expect consistent evaluations across conditions for visual cues, such as color. However, it remains to be tested whether consumers can assess structural or haptic attributes in VR, such as material, or texture, in the absence of physical touch. Structural elements, for instance, are typically evaluated through visual, haptic, and motor input (Festila & Chrysochou, 2018), and their perception may differ in virtual contexts. In online and VR settings, the inability to touch products can affect consumers' responses, especially for products whose material properties are central to decision-making (Briand Decré & Cloonan, 2019). Although VR offers a high level of immersion, touch remains absent, which may impact how cues like material (structural cue) and texture (haptic cue) are processed. Moreover, even if product evaluations in VR align with those in PR, it is still unclear whether they lead to comparable attitudinal or behavioral outcomes.

A secondary goal of this study is to identify which packaging alternatives, across the structural, haptic, and visual manipulations, elicit the most favorable attitudinal responses.

This research aims to contribute in three ways:

(a) theoretically, by examining whether VR elicits consumer behavior consistent with PR and identifying any significant differences, and providing information on the sustainability assessment of different packaging alternatives;
(b) methodologically, by offering insights into the design and conduct of consumer experiments in VR settings;
(c) empirically, by providing actionable implications for managers and practitioners on the use of VR as a product testing and design environment, and to design sustainable packaging.

4.2 Hypotheses Development

Since the main goal of this research is to unveil consumers' responses to packaging in VR and differences with PR, different measures should be compared and analyzed. To this end, the empirical analysis will focus on a wide spectrum of dependent variables, such as:

- perceived sustainability (PS);
- willingness to pay a premium price (WTPP);
- purchase intention (PI);
- attitude toward packaging (ATP);
- perceived quality (PQ);
- attractiveness (ATT).

To ensure a comprehensive understanding of consumer responses, comparing VR and PR involves more than assessing differences in average scores for each dependent variable. It also requires examining how various packaging cues (structural, haptic, and visual) are evaluated across conditions, and whether the relative ranking or preference order of packaging alternatives remains consistent between VR and PR. This approach allows for a deeper analysis of both the magnitude and the direction of consumers' responses across immersive and physical environments.

Thus, two sets of hypotheses are proposed for this research. The first set (higher-order hypotheses) aims to compare consumer responses across VR and PR environments. The second set (lower-order hypotheses) focuses on specific comparisons between the packaging alternatives within each condition (VR and PR), across different attitudinal measures.

Collectively, these hypotheses are presented in Table 4.1.

4.2.1 Hypotheses About Virtual Reality and Physical Reality Comparison

In formulating higher-order hypotheses that posit similar consumer responses in VR and PR environments, this research aligns with a growing body of evidence supporting VR's capacity to simulate real-world evaluations. Interaction in VR is realistic and generates a strong sense of presence (e.g., Flavián et al., 2021; Hilken et al., 2022; Kang et al., 2020; Loureiro et al., 2019). Besides offering new shopping experiences (Luna-Nevarez & McGovern, 2021), VR is also very suitable for conducting product testing and prototyping (Hube et al., 2020). Studies like Peukert et al. (2019) have found that product evaluation in VR closely resembles that in PR. In the realm of food products, VR provides realistic cues and drives natural product research (Huang et al., 2021). Consumers in a VR store exhibit similar shopping patterns and behaviors to those in PR, with minor differences in product evaluation (e.g., Schnack et al., 2020; Siegrist et al., 2019). Moreover, VR offers participants a better and more comprehensive understanding of products, with minor differences observed between high- and low-immersive experiences (Naderi et al., 2020). Branca et al. (2023) tested several packaging manipulations, finding similar results for willingness to pay premium and perceived sustainability across VR and PR. Pfeiffer et al. (2020) highlight some similarities between virtual and physical supermarkets, calling for research that contrasts VR with PR.

Despite the lack of haptic feedback, which remains a current limitation of VR, the ability of VR to visually replicate complex packaging stimuli has improved significantly thanks to technological advancements. VR can simulate real products and enable users to experience haptic-like interactions, even without physical contact (Alzayat & Lee, 2021; Branca et al., 2023). Haptic cues, even when individuals cannot physically touch the product, remain relevant for product evaluation (Cowan et al., 2021).

For these reasons, and given the limited yet promising empirical foundation, the present research adopts a conservative approach by hypothesizing similar consumer responses in VR and PR for the constructs investigated.

Table 4.1 Overview of research hypotheses

H1. Consumers show a similar level of packaging perceived sustainability in Virtual Reality and Physical Reality	
H2. Consumers show a similar level of willingness to pay a premium price in Virtual Reality and Physical Reality	
H3. Consumers show a similar level of purchase intention in Virtual Reality and Physical Reality	
H4. Consumers show a similar level of attitude toward the packaging in Virtual Reality and Physical Reality	
H5. Consumers show a similar level of perceived quality in Virtual Reality and Physical Reality	
H6. Consumers show a similar level of packaging attractiveness in Virtual Reality and Physical Reality	
Structural cues	H-PS1. Glass packaging is perceived as more sustainable than carton packaging, which in turn is perceived as more sustainable than plastic packaging
	H-WTPP1. Consumers are willing to pay a premium price for glass packaging over carton packaging, and for carton packaging over plastic packaging
	H-PI1. Glass packaging elicits higher purchase intention over carton packaging, and carton packaging over plastic packaging
	H-ATP1. Glass packaging elicits a higher attitude toward packaging over carton packaging, and carton packaging over plastic packaging
	H-PQ1. Glass packaging elicits a higher perceived quality over carton packaging, and carton packaging over plastic packaging
	H-ATT1. Glass packaging elicits a higher attractiveness over carton packaging, and carton packaging over plastic packaging
Haptic cues	H-PS2. Rough packaging is perceived as more sustainable than normal packaging, which in turn is perceived as more sustainable than smooth packaging
	H-WTPP2. Consumers are willing to pay a premium price for rough packaging over normal packaging, and for normal packaging over smooth packaging
	H-PI2. Rough packaging elicits higher purchase intention over normal packaging, and normal packaging over smooth packaging
	H-ATP2. Rough packaging elicits a higher attitude toward packaging over normal packaging, and normal packaging over smooth packaging
	H-PQ2. Rough packaging elicits a higher perceived quality over normal packaging, and normal packaging over smooth packaging
	H-ATT2. Rough packaging elicits a higher attractiveness over normal packaging, and normal packaging over smooth packaging
Visual cues	H-PS3. Green packaging is perceived as more sustainable than beige packaging, which in turn is perceived as more sustainable than blue packaging
	H-WTPP3. Consumers are willing to pay a premium price for green packaging over beige packaging, and for beige packaging over blue packaging
	H-PI3. Green packaging elicits higher purchase intention over beige packaging, and beige packaging over blue packaging
	H-ATP3. Green packaging elicits a higher attitude toward packaging over beige packaging, and beige packaging over blue packaging

(continued)

Table 4.1 (continued)

	H-PQ3. Green packaging elicits a higher perceived quality over beige packaging, and beige packaging over blue packaging
	H-ATT3. Green packaging elicits a higher attractiveness over beige packaging, and beige packaging over blue packaging

H1. Consumers show a similar level of packaging perceived sustainability in Virtual Reality and Physical Reality.

H2. Consumers show a similar level of willingness to pay a premium price in Virtual Reality and Physical Reality.

H3. Consumers show a similar level of purchase intention in Virtual Reality and Physical Reality.

H4. Consumers show a similar level of attitude toward the packaging in Virtual Reality and Physical Reality.

H5. Consumers show a similar level of perceived quality in Virtual Reality and Physical Reality.

H6. Consumers show a similar level of packaging attractiveness in Virtual Reality and Physical Reality.

4.2.2 Hypotheses About Packaging Evaluation

Recent studies highlight how consumers' perception is mainly influenced by packaging material and structure (e.g., Herbes et al., 2020; Scott & Vigar-Ellis, 2014; Steenis et al., 2017), but their evaluation is generally not aligned, or even opposite, with the actual LCA and environmental impact (e.g., Boesen et al., 2019; Herbes et al., 2018, 2020; Steenis et al., 2017). Glass and bioplastic are perceived as the most sustainable solution, followed by laminated cartons and plastic (Boesen et al., 2019). According to Steenis et al. (2017), consumers consider glass as the greener solution, followed by the liquid carton, plastic pouch, mixed pouch, dry carton sachet and can. Similarly, Nguyen et al. (2020) found that paper is deemed to be the most eco-friendly alternative. According to what emerged in the previous literature, it is possible to hypothesize that a glass package is perceived as a more sustainable solution, compared to a cardboard package of the same product, and that plastic packaging is perceived as the least sustainable. Thus, it is hypothesized that:

H-PS1. Glass packaging is perceived as more sustainable than carton packaging, which in turn is perceived as more sustainable than plastic packaging.

When it comes to sensory cues, i.e., the perception of touch and feel, natural materials are associated with eco-friendliness (Karana, 2012; Karana & Nijkamp, 2014). An opaque, rough, non-reflective material is associated with naturalness, differently from a smooth, reflective, glossy one. Magnier & Schoormans (2017) also highlighted how packaging made of fiber-based material has a higher perceived sustainability than a plastic one. Based on the above, rough packaging is expected to be perceived as more sustainable than normal packaging, and smooth packaging to be perceived as the least sustainable.

H-PS2. Rough packaging is perceived as more sustainable than normal packaging, which in turn is perceived as more sustainable than smooth packaging.

Felix et al. (2021) show that research about the packaging color effect on marketing variables, in relation to eco-friendly products, is scarce, in line with Seo and Scammon (2017), who highlight how color has not received much attention in green product studies. Consumers generally can use earth colors (such as cream, brown, or green) to assess packaging as eco-friendly (Scott & Vigar-Ellis, 2014). Pancer et al. (2017) highlight that a green packaging leads to a higher perceived sustainability than a black or white one. Even though the color green is generally associated with eco-friendliness and conscious consumption (Labrecque et al., 2013), green seems not to be always the best color to convey sustainability, according to Barchiesi et al. (2018). They found that blue is preferable to convey CSR messages. Differently, in Sundar and Kellaris (2017) visual exposure to green or blue colors triggers a similar perception of eco-friendliness. While Seo and Scammon (2017) claim that the color green enhances perceptions of the brand's environmental impact when the packaging includes an environmental claim, Samaraweera et al. (2021) found that a predominantly white-toned label works better than a green-toned one for eco-friendly products. Marozzo et al. (2020) found that au naturel colors, which include hues of beige, e.g., cream, sandy beiges, and mellow browns, are considered natural, organic, earthy, and eco-friendly. Since there appear to be conflicting indications in the previous literature, conservative hypotheses about visual cues are formulated in this research.

H-PS3. Green packaging is perceived as more sustainable than beige packaging, which in turn is perceived as more sustainable than blue packaging.

Several studies analyze the willingness to pay for green products and eco-packaging, with mixed results. A stream of research argues that consumers show a higher willingness to pay a premium price (WTPP) for sustainable packaging. Nguyen et al. (2020) point out that consumers show WTPP if they are satisfied with the characteristics of the market's appeal. Even if consumers' actual behavior is generally inconsistent with their attitudes, they usually show a WTPP for eco-friendly products (Vecchio & Annunziata, 2015). Packaging perceived to be sustainable may lead consumers to WTPP for the product, because of the positive association triggered by the packaging. Singh and Pandey (2018) analyze the WTPP for green packaging as a proxy of actual behavior. Moser (2015) finds that willingness to pay is the strongest predictor of green purchasing behavior. According to a different line of research, consumers perceive green packaging as more expensive and some of them are not willing to pay an extra price (Magnier & Crié, 2015). In general, they show WTPP for socially responsible products, but for those that benefit humans over those that benefit the environment (Tully & Winer, 2014). Among other CSR claims, green packaging is the lowest in WTPP, according to Aagerup et al. (2019) and Wei et al. (2018). Even if recyclable packaging is the strongest in influencing purchase intention, it is the weakest in generating added value, compared to other ethical attributes (Mai, 2014). Buyers are not willing to pay more for a green package, regardless of the presence of other labels or claims (Ertz et al., 2017). Even considering some mixed previous findings, it is assumed that packaging deemed more sustainable leads to a higher WTPP than one considered less sustainable. Based on the above, it is hypothesized that:

H-WTPP1. Consumers are willing to pay a premium price for glass packaging over carton packaging, and for carton packaging over plastic packaging.

H-WTPP2. Consumers are willing to pay a premium price for rough packaging over normal packaging, and for normal packaging over smooth packaging.

H-WTPP3. Consumers are willing to pay a premium price for green packaging over beige packaging, and for beige packaging over blue packaging.

As highlighted by Steenis et al. (2017), packaging sustainability plays a significant role in consumers' intention to purchase. Green packaging was found to be positively related to purchase intention in Trivedi et al. (2018), in line with the eco-friendly packaging claim, which was found to positively influence purchase intention in Wei et al. (2018). According to Magnier and Schoormans (2015), the ecological visual appearance of the packaging positively influences intention to purchase. If marketers highlight the environmental benefits associated with eco-friendly packaging, purchase intention and attitudes can be positively influenced (Prakash et al., 2019). Interestingly, the overpackaging elimination (i.e., a more sustainable alternative) reduces purchase intention only if consumers are not environmentally conscious and if they are facing competing overpackaged products (Monnot et al., 2019). Rees et al. (2019), however, found that sustainability cues on the packaging have a limited translation from recognition to insinuated purchasing intention. Jerzyk (2016) claims that green packaging may be of little importance in young consumers' purchase decisions, but they show a willingness to change behavior if sustainable packaging messages are credible. In this light, it is assumed that a packaging solution deemed as more sustainable leads to a higher purchase intention than one considered as less sustainable. Thus, it is hypothesized that:

H-PI1. Glass packaging elicits higher purchase intention over carton packaging, and carton packaging over plastic packaging.

H-PI2. Rough packaging elicits higher purchase intention over normal packaging, and normal packaging over smooth packaging.

H-PI3. Green packaging elicits higher purchase intention over beige packaging, and beige packaging over blue packaging.

Previous research suggests that consumers have a positive attitude toward more sustainable packaging (Steenis et al., 2018). Attitude toward packaging refers to the consumers' feeling of favorability of the packaging (Holmes & Paswan, 2012). Attitude affects behavioral intentions, which in turn shape actual behavior (Hernandez-Fernandez et al., 2022; Shimul & Cheah, 2023). Trivedi et al. (2018) claimed that packaging constitutes an important determinant in purchase intention and, in line with Rokka and Uusitalo (2008), attitude toward packaging should be analyzed as a factor of consumer choice modeling. According to Prakash et al. (2019), consumers prefer eco-friendly packaged products, whereas non-recyclable packaging negatively influences their attitudes toward the usage of such products. Hence, it is hypothesized that:

H-ATP1. Glass packaging elicits a higher attitude toward packaging over carton packaging, carton packaging over plastic packaging.

H-ATP2. Rough packaging elicits a higher attitude toward packaging over normal packaging, and normal packaging over smooth packaging.

H-ATP3. Green packaging elicits a higher attitude toward packaging over beige packaging, and beige packaging over blue packaging.

Perceived quality may be intended as the way consumers value a product's equity and superiority compared to the available alternatives (Beneke et al., 2013), representing a variable of great interest (Briand Decré & Cloonan, 2019). Quality perceptions precede overall evaluations (Söderlund et al., 2017). In the store, consumers first encounter the packaging before the product itself. Then, if shoppers have more direct experience handling the packaging, they are more likely to infer the perceived quality of the packaging to the product itself (Holmes & Paswan, 2012). Packaging material and surface can affect the product perceived quality. Touch sensation can be a more relevant variable in the perceived product quality compared to the price, even for packaging (Briand Decré & Cloonan, 2019). Positive environmental messages can enhance perceived quality (Borin et al., 2011; Ertz et al., 2017), and even food safety (Donato & D'Aniello, 2022). Attributes associated with naturalness, such as roughness, opacity, or visible fibers, are linked to higher evaluations of both sustainability and quality (Karana, 2012). Indeed, the literature suggests that sustainable packaging communicates product quality (e.g., Binninger, 2017; Magnier et al., 2016). Based on the above, it is hypothesized that:

H-PQ1. Glass packaging elicits a higher perceived quality over carton packaging, and carton packaging over plastic packaging.

H-PQ2. Rough packaging elicits a higher perceived quality over normal packaging, and normal packaging over smooth packaging.

H-PQ3. Green packaging elicits a higher perceived quality over beige packaging, and beige packaging over blue packaging.

Attractiveness refers to considering a stimulus as attractive, pleasing, or likable (Giese et al., 2014). Visual appeal is an important element in packaging design because attractiveness guides consumer behavior, capturing attention, generating liking, creating value and supporting brand positioning (Orth & Crouch, 2014). Attractiveness can be considered a technical quality of packaging that represents an important factor at the purchase moment (Briand Decré & Cloonan, 2019). Moreover, the aesthetic appeal of a design constitutes a hedonic benefit (Giese et al., 2014) and can be a starting point for the formation of a bond between consumer and brand (Orth & Crouch, 2014). Attractiveness enhances purchase intention by increasing the perceived value. Thus, a consumer who perceives two offers as similar on the utilitarian side tends to purchase the more attractive alternative (Giese et al., 2014).

Finally, Granato et al. (2022) show that eco-packaging can increase aesthetic quality perception. Although there is no substantial literature addressing the issue of the attractiveness of sustainable packaging, in line with the above, it is hypothesized that:

H-ATT1. Glass packaging elicits a higher attractiveness over carton packaging, and carton packaging over plastic packaging.

H-ATT2. Rough packaging elicits a higher attractiveness over normal packaging, and normal packaging over smooth packaging.

H-ATT3. Green packaging elicits a higher attractiveness over beige packaging, and beige packaging over blue packaging.

4.2.3 Overview of Research Hypotheses

Table 4.1 shows a complete overview of the hypotheses tested in the current research. First, the VR vs. PR high-order hypotheses are presented, followed by the packaging sustainability low-order hypotheses, organized according to the different types of cues.

4.3 Research Design

Before the main experiment, a preliminary study was conducted. In this case, designed packaging manipulation and stimuli were examined, to collect preliminary feedback on the direction of the research hypotheses. Two focus groups were conducted since the interest was in the interaction between the participants and in a perspective not expressed by numbers, which differs from the answers obtained from the main study (Millward, 2012).

A mixed between-within-subjects design experiment was carried out as the main empirical analysis. The between-subject design was chosen since the aim was to compare consumer behavior in VR and PR and prevent the assessment from being influenced by previous experiences. The within-subject design was chosen to mimic a realistic shopping experience (Aagerup et al., 2019; Cho & Baskin, 2018): during the purchase process, consumers generally see several products, one after the other. The experiment is a 2 (VR vs. PR) × 7 (packaging manipulations) laboratory experiment, and it can be ideally divided into three studies since there are three groups of manipulations that have in common the control group, namely a blue carton packaging (baseline). Details about the stimuli development process are presented in Sect. 4.4. From this point on, we will refer to:

- Study 1 for a 2 (VR vs. PR) × 3 (structural cues) between-within-subjects experiment;
- Study 2 for a 2 (VR vs. PR) × 3 (haptic cues) between-within-subjects experiment; and

- Study 3 for a 2 (VR vs. PR) × 3 (visual cues) between-within-subjects experiment.

The process, the samples, part of the manipulations and investigated relations are in common with Branca et al. (2023), of which this research represents a continuation and extension.

4.4 Stimuli Development

Food and beverage was selected as the product category. For FMCGs, the role of packaging visual elements is essential (Chrysochou & Festila, 2019). During low-involvement situations, such as food choice, packaging design elements become particularly effective, since consumers use these heuristics to simplify their decisions (Festila & Chrysochou, 2018). This research focuses on differences across packaging elements while the product does not change, that is, extrinsic packaging attributes rather than intrinsic product attributes (Orth & Crouch, 2014). Thus, the product choice should not have a major effect on the results (in line with Liao et al., 2015).

Specifically, we selected milk packaging for several reasons: it is a widely available consumer product sold in various retail settings, characterized by a relatively straightforward purchasing decision process (Peukert et al., 2019), and it is available in a large variety of packaging alternatives (Littel & Orth, 2013; Orth & Crouch, 2014). Moreover, milk is a product commonly purchased for personal use or on behalf of others, ensuring familiarity with the product (Boesen et al., 2019). Examples of the use of milk in packaging and sustainability research can also be found in Boesen et al. (2019) and Wei et al. (2018).

To prevent any prior product knowledge from influencing participants, increase the realism of the study and allow precise manipulations, we opted to create new mock-ups of a fictitious milk product, rather than using an existing market product (Liao et al., 2015; Machiels & Orth, 2017; Seo & Scammon, 2017; Söderlund et al., 2017). Collaborating with two experienced graphic designers (as in Liao et al., 2015), we developed a digital mock-up of a baseline packaging, building on the alternatives already available in the Italian market, where the research has been conducted, to enhance the realism of the stimuli. This design featured a common blue color, typical of milk packaging in the Italian market, and employed the carton as the baseline material, consistent with standard liquid food packaging. The package displayed simple text in Italian, such as "*latte intero*" (whole milk) and "*1 litro*" (1 liter), to contextualize the product's contents for the participants, in line with previous research in non-English speaking countries (e.g., Aagerup et al., 2019; Huang et al., 2021; Meißner et al., 2020). Finally, the minimal design recalls a drop of milk. This process is in line with Söderlund et al. (2017), who stressed the importance of the representativeness of the stimuli, trying to represent actual occurrences in real shopping situations. The creative process is shown in Fig. 4.1 (Branca et al., 2023).

Building on this baseline version, three groups of manipulation were carried out, while keeping fixed verbal information on the packaging.

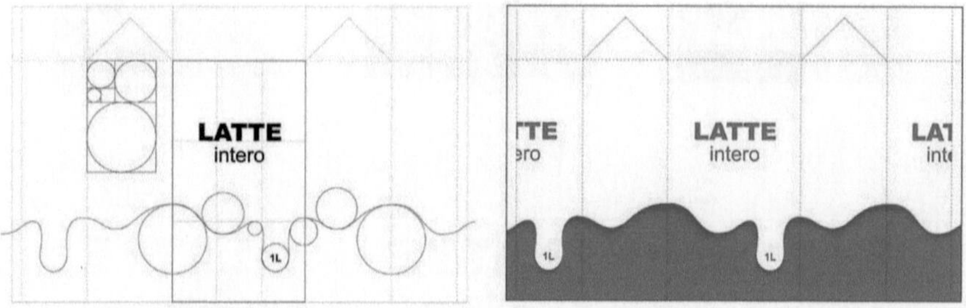

Fig. 4.1 The creative process for stimuli design (Branca et al., 2023)

Fig. 4.2 The labels of the glass and plastic bottles

In the first group, we altered the packaging material, selecting common structural designs, namely a glass bottle and a plastic bottle (Boesen et al., 2019; Chrysochou & Festila, 2019; Steenis et al., 2017). For the glass and plastic bottles, ad hoc labels were realized, identical to the baseline packaging design, as shown in Fig. 4.2.

The second group of manipulations concerned the haptic cues. Modifying the cardboard composition of the baseline packaging, a rough, non-reflective, opaque, warm packaging, and a smooth, reflective, glossy, cold alternative were realized (Briand Decré & Cloonan, 2019; Chen, 2021; Karana, 2012; Karana & Nijkamp, 2014; Littel & Orth, 2013).

In the third group, we introduced color variations (Barchiesi et al., 2018; Festila & Chrysochou, 2018). Starting from the blue baseline packaging, a green version, and a beige one (inspired by Marozzo et al., 2020) were realized. Saturation and color brightness were kept constant (Liao et al., 2015). This process resulted in a total of seven distinct packaging alternatives across the three manipulation groups, all sharing the same blue baseline carton packaging. A summary is presented in Fig. 4.3.

After the preliminary study, minor changes were made. The final versions were then produced in collaboration with two partner companies, respectively specializing in cardboard packaging production and VR applications. White-label packaging was purchased for the glass and plastic bottles. This process yielded seven physical versions of the milk packaging, each corresponding to a VR counterpart, ensuring identical representations.

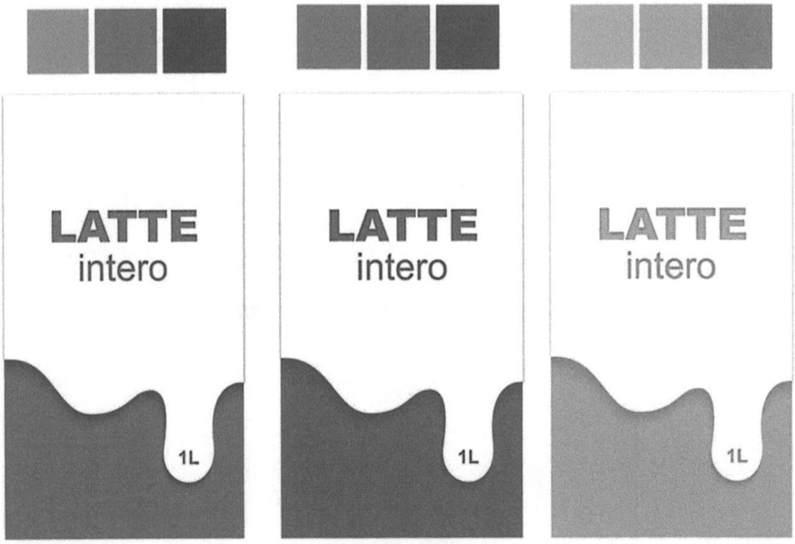

Fig. 4.3 Details of the visual cues' manipulations

Therefore, we obtained seven physical versions of the milk packaging and seven perfectly identical versions in VR, as shown in Figs. 4.4, 4.5, and 4.6.

For the main experiment, we created a neutral VR environment characterized by minimal aesthetics and neutral colors, mirroring a neutral physical room used for the experiments in PR. In both settings, a central table displayed one packaging mock-up at the time, maintaining consistency between the virtual and physical procedures.

4.5 Measurements

All dependent variables were operationalized in a questionnaire by using scales adapted from previous literature. An overview is presented in Table 4.2.

Fig. 4.4 Plastic bottle, baseline packaging, and glass bottle, in PR and VR (Branca et al., 2023)

Fig. 4.5 Rough packaging, baseline packaging, and smooth packaging, in PR and VR (Branca et al., 2023)

Fig. 4.6 Beige packaging, baseline packaging, and green packaging, in PR and VR

Table 4.2 Scale measurements

Construct	Response scale	Items	Scale/item origins
Perceived sustainability	7-point (1 = strongly disagree, 7 = strongly agree)	This milk pack is environmentally friendly A person who cares about the environment would be likely to buy this milk pack	Gershoff and Frels (2015)
Willingness to pay a premium price	7-point (1 = strongly disagree, 7 = strongly agree)	I am ready to pay a higher price for this milk pack Buying this milk pack seems smart to me even if it costs more	Chaudhuri and Holbrook (2001)
Purchase intention	7-point (1 = very low, 7 = very high)	My intention to purchase this milk pack is… The likelihood that I would buy this milk pack, if available, is…	Dodds et al. (1991)
Attitude toward packaging	7-point (1 = negative, 7 = positive)	My general evaluation of this milk pack is…	Crites et al. (1994)
Perceived quality	7-point (1 = low quality, 7 = good quality)	All things considered, I would say that this milk pack is globally of…	Sprott and Shimp (2004)
Attractiveness	7-point semantic different scale (1 = unattractive, 7 = attractive)	This milk pack is…	Magnier et al. (2016)

References

Aagerup, U., Frank, A. S., & Hultqvist, E. (2019). The persuasive effects of emotional green packaging claims. *British Food Journal, 121*(12), 3233–3246. https://doi.org/10.1108/BFJ-08-2019-0652

Akturan, U., Kuter, D., & Gökkut, B. S. (2025). Mirror, mirror on the wall, who is the most convincing of them all? A systematic literature review on packaging. *Journal of Business Research, 193*, Article 115355. https://doi.org/10.1016/j.jbusres.2025.115355

Alzayat, A., & Lee, S. H. M. (2021). Virtual products as an extension of my body: Exploring hedonic and utilitarian shopping value in a virtual reality retail environment. *Journal of Business Research, 130*, 348–363. https://doi.org/10.1016/j.jbusres.2021.03.017

Barchiesi, M. A., Castellan, S., & Costa, R. (2018). In the eye of the beholder: Communicating CSR through color in packaging design. *Journal of Marketing Communications, 24*(7), 720–733. https://doi.org/10.1080/13527266.2016.1224771

Beneke, J., Flynn, R., Greig, T., & Mukaiwa, M. (2013). The influence of perceived product quality, relative price and risk on customer value and willingness to buy: A study of private label merchandise. *Journal of Product & Brand Management, 22*(3), 218–228. https://doi.org/10.1108/JPBM-02-2013-0262

Binninger, A. S. (2017). Perception of naturalness of food packaging and its role in consumer product evaluation. *Journal of Food Products Marketing, 23*(3), 251–266. https://doi.org/10.1080/10454446.2014.885868

Boesen, S., Bey, N., & Niero, M. (2019). Environmental sustainability of liquid food packaging. Is there a gap between Danish consumers' perception and learnings from life cycle assessment? *Journal of Cleaner Production, 210*, 1193–1206. https://doi.org/10.1016/j.jclepro.2018.11.055

Borin, N., Cerf, D. C., & Krishnan, R. (2011). Consumer effects of environmental impact in product labelling. *Journal of Consumer Marketing, 28*(1), 76–86. https://doi.org/10.1108/07363761111101976

Branca, G., Resciniti, R., & Loureiro, S. M. C. (2023). Virtual is so real! Consumers' evaluation of product packaging in virtual reality. *Psychology & Marketing, 40*, 596–609. https://doi.org/10.1002/mar.21743

Briand Decré, G., & Cloonan, C. (2019). A touch of gloss: Haptic perception of packaging and consumers' reactions. *Journal of Product & Brand Management, 28*(1), 117–132. https://doi.org/10.1108/JPBM-05-2017-1472

Chaudhuri, A., & Holbrook, M. B. (2001). The Chain of Effects from Brand Trust and Brand Affect to Brand Performance: The Role of Brand Loyalty. *Journal of Marketing, 65*(2), 81–93. https://doi.org/10.1509/jmkg.65.2.81.18255

Chen, Y. S. A. (2021). Does outward appearance appeal to the inward mind? The impact of packaging finishes on brand impressions and the subsequent behavior of consumer. *Journal of Product & Brand Management, 30*(5), 768–778. https://doi.org/10.1108/JPBM-07-2019-2466

Chen, H., Li, H., & Pirkkalainen, H. (2024). How extended reality influences e-commerce consumers: A literature review. *Electronic Commerce Research and Applications, 65*, Article 101404. https://doi.org/10.1016/j.elerap.2024.101404

Cho, Y. N., & Baskin, E. (2018). It's a match when green meets healthy in sustainability labelling. *Journal of Business Research, 86*, 119–129. https://doi.org/10.1016/j.jbusres.2018.01.050

Cowan, K., Spielmann, N., Horn, E., & Griffart, C. (2021). Perception is reality… How digital retail environments influence brand perceptions through presence. *Journal of Business Research, 123*, 86–96. https://doi.org/10.1016/j.jbusres.2020.09.058

Chrysochou, P., & Festila, A. (2019). A content analysis of organic product package designs. *Journal of Consumer Marketing, 36*(4), 441–448. https://doi.org/10.1108/JCM-06-2018-2720

Crites, S. L., Fabrigar, L. R., & Petty, R. E. (1994). Measuring the affective and cognitive properties of attitudes: Conceptual and methodological issues. *Personality and Social Psychology Bulletin, 20*(6), 619–634. https://doi.org/10.1177/0146167294206001

Dodds, W. B., Monroe, K. B., & Grewal, D. (1991). Effects of price, brand, and store information on buyers' product evaluations. *Journal of Marketing Research, 28*(3), 307–319. https://doi.org/10.1177/002224379102800305

Donato, C., & D'Aniello, A. (2022). Tell me more and make me feel proud: The role of eco-labels and informational cues on consumers' food perceptions. *British Food Journal, 124*(4), 1365–1382. https://doi.org/10.1108/BFJ-04-2021-0416

Ertz, M., François, J., & Durif, F. (2017). How consumers react to environmental information. An experimental study. *Journal of International Consumer Marketing, 29*(3), 162–178. https://doi.org/10.1080/08961530.2016.1273813.

Felix, R., González, E. M., Castaño, R., Carrete, L., & Gretz, R. T. (2021). When the green in green packaging backfires: Gender effects and perceived masculinity of environmentally friendly products. *International Journal of Consumer Studies, 00*, 1–19. https://doi.org/10.1111/ijcs.12738

Festila, A., & Chrysochou, P. (2018). Implicit communication of food product healthfulness through package design: A content analysis. *Journal of Consumer Behavior, 17*, 461–476. https://doi.org/10.1002/cb.1732

Flavián, C., Ibáñez-Sánchez, S., & Orús, C. (2021). Impacts of technological embodiment through virtual reality on potential guests' emotions and engagement. *Journal of Hospitality Marketing and Management, 30*(1), 1–20. https://doi.org/10.1080/19368623.2020.1770146

Gershoff, A. D., & Frels, J. K. (2015). What makes it green? The role of centrality of green attributes in evaluations of the greenness of products. *Journal of Marketing, 79*(1), 97–110. https://doi.org/10.1509/jm.13.0303

Giese, J. L., Malkewitz, K., Orth, U. R., & Henderson, P. W. (2014). Advancing the aesthetic middle principle: Trade-offs in design attractiveness and strength. *Journal of Business Research, 67*(6), 1154–1161. https://doi.org/10.1016/j.jbusres.2013.05.018

Granato, G., Fischer, A. H. R., & van Trijp, H. C. M. (2022). The price of sustainability: How consumers trade-off conventional packaging benefits against sustainability. *Journal of Cleaner Production, 365*, Article 132739. https://doi.org/10.1016/j.jclepro.2022.132739

Herbes, C., Beuthner, C., & Ramme, I. (2018). Consumer attitudes towards biobased packaging. A cross-cultural comparative study. *Journal of Cleaner Production, 194*(1), 203–218. https://doi.org/10.1016/j.jclepro.2018.05.106

Herbes, C., Beuthner, C., & Ramme, I. (2020). How green is your packaging - A comparative international study of cues consumers use to recognize environmentally friendly packaging. *International Journal of Consumer Studies, 44*(3), 258–271. https://doi.org/10.1111/ijcs.12560

Hernandez-Fernandez, A., Kuster-Boluda, I., & Vila-Lopez, N. (2022). Nutritional information labels and health claims to promote healthy consumption. *Journal of Business & Industrial Marketing, 37*(8), 1650–1661. https://doi.org/10.1108/JBIM-09-2020-0426

Hilken, T., Chylinski, M., Keeling, D. I., Heller, J., Ruyter, K., & Mahr, D. (2022). How to strategically choose or combine augmented and virtual reality for improved online experiential retailing. *Psychology & Marketing, 39*, 495–507. https://doi.org/10.1002/mar.21600

Holmes, G. R., & Paswan, A. (2012). Consumer reaction to new package design. *Journal of Product & Brand Management, 21*(2), 109–116. https://doi.org/10.1108/10610421211215553

Huang, J., Zhao, P., & Wan, X. (2021). From brain variations to individual differences in the color–flavor incongruency effect: A combined virtual reality and resting-state fMRI study. *Journal of Business Research, 123*, 604–612. https://doi.org/10.1016/j.jbusres.2020.10.031

Hube, N., Müller, M., Lapczyna, E., & Wojdziak, J. (2020). Mixed Reality based collaboration for design processes. *i-com, 19*(2), 123–137. https://doi.org/10.1515/icom-2020-0012.

Jerzyk, E. (2016). Design and communication of ecological content on sustainable packaging in young consumers' opinions. *Journal of Food Products Marketing, 22*(6), 707–716. https://doi.org/10.1080/10454446.2015.1121435

Kang, H. J., Shin, J., & Ponto, K. (2020). How 3D Virtual Reality stores can shape consumer purchase decisions: The roles of informativeness and playfulness. *Journal of Interactive Marketing, 49*, 70–85. https://doi.org/10.1016/j.intmar.2019.07.002

Karana, E. (2012). Characterization of 'natural' and 'high-quality' materials to improve perception of bio-plastics. *Journal of Cleaner Production, 37*, 316–325. https://doi.org/10.1016/j.jclepro.2012.07.034

Karana, E., & Nijkamp, N. (2014). Fiberness, reflectiveness and roughness in the characterization of natural and high quality materials. *Journal of Cleaner Production, 68*, 252–260. https://doi.org/10.1016/j.jclepro.2014.01.001

Labrecque, L. I., Patrick, V. M., & Milne, G. R. (2013). The marketers' prismatic palette: A review of color research and future directions. *Psychology & Marketing, 30*(2), 187–202. https://doi.org/10.1002/mar.20597

Liao, L. L., Corsi, A. M., Chrysochou, P., & Larry Lockshin, L. (2015). Emotional responses towards food packaging: A joint application of self-report and physiological measures of emotion. *Food Quality and Preference, 42*, 48–55. https://doi.org/10.1016/j.foodqual.2015.01.009

Littel, S., & Orth, U. R. (2013). Effects of package visuals and haptics on brand evaluations. *European Journal of Marketing, 47*(1/2), 198–217. https://doi.org/10.1108/03090561311285510

Loureiro, S. M. C., Guerreiro, J., Eloy, E., Langaro, D., & Panchapakesan, P. (2019). Understanding the use of Virtual Reality in Marketing: A text mining-based review. *Journal of Business Research, 100*, 514–530. https://doi.org/10.1016/j.jbusres.2018.10.055

Luna-Nevarez, C., & McGovern, E. (2021). The rise of the virtual reality (VR) marketplace: Exploring the antecedents and consequences of consumer attitudes toward V-Commerce. *Journal of Internet Commerce, 20*(2), 167–194. https://doi.org/10.1080/15332861.2021.1875766

Machiels, C. J. A., & Orth, U. R. (2017). Verticality in product labels and shelves as a metaphorical cue to quality. *Journal of Retailing and Consumer Services, 37*, 195–203. https://doi.org/10.1016/j.jretconser.2017.02.009

Mai, L. W. (2014). Consumers' willingness to pay for ethical attributes. *Marketing Intelligence & Planning, 32*(6), 706–721. https://doi.org/10.1108/MIP-08-2013-0139

Magnier, L., & Crié, D. (2015). Communicating packaging eco-friendliness: An exploration of consumers' perceptions of eco-designed packaging. *International Journal of Retail & Distribution Management, 43*(4/5), 350–366. https://doi.org/10.1108/IJRDM-04-2014-0048

Magnier, L., & Schoormans, J. (2015). Consumer reactions to sustainable packaging: The interplay of visual appearance, verbal claim and environmental concern. *Journal of Environmental Psychology, 44*, 53–62. https://doi.org/10.1016/j.jenvp.2015.09.005

Magnier, L., Schoormans, J., & Mugge, R. (2016). Judging a product by its cover. Packaging sustainability and perceptions of quality in food products. *Food Quality and Preference, 53*, 132–142. https://doi.org/10.1016/j.foodqual.2016.06.006

Magnier, L., & Schoormans, J. (2017). How do packaging material, colour and environmental claim influence package, brand and product evaluations? *Packaging Technology and Science, 30*(11), 735–751. https://doi.org/10.1002/pts.2318

Marozzo, V., Raimondo, M. A., Miceli, G. "Nino," & Scopelliti, I. (2020). Effects of au naturel packaging colors on willingness to pay for healthy food. *Psychology & Marketing, 37*(7), 913–927. https://doi.org/10.1002/mar.21294

Meißner, M., Pfeiffer, J., Peukert, C., Dietrich, H., & Pfeiffer, T. (2020). How virtual reality affects consumer choice. *Journal of Business Research, 117*, 219–231. https://doi.org/10.1016/j.jbusres.2020.06.004

Millward, L. (2012). Focus groups. In G. M. Breakwell, J. A. Smith, & D. B. Wright (Eds.), *Research Methods in Psychology* (4th ed.). Sage.

Monnot, E., Reniou, F., Parguel, B., & Elgaaïed-Gambier, L. (2019). Thinking outside the packaging box: Should brands consider store shelf context when eliminating overpackaging? *Journal of Business Ethics, 154*, 355–370. https://doi.org/10.1007/s10551-017-3439-0

Moser, A. K. (2015). Thinking green, buying green? Drivers of pro - Environmental purchasing behavior. *Journal of Consumer Marketing, 32*(3), 167–175. https://doi.org/10.1108/JCM-10-2014-1179

Naderi, E., Naderi, I., & Balakrishnan, B. (2020). Product design matters, but is it enough? Consumers' responses to product design and environment congruence. *Journal of Product & Brand Management, 29*(7), 939–954. https://doi.org/10.1108/JPBM-08-2018-1975

Nguyen, A. T., Parker, L., Brennan, L., & Lockrey, S. (2020). A consumer definition of eco-friendly packaging. *Journal of Cleaner Production, 252*, Article 119792. https://doi.org/10.1016/j.jclepro.2019.119792

Orth, U. R., & Crouch, R. C. (2014). Is beauty in the aisles of the retailer? Package processing in visually complex contexts. *Journal of Retailing, 90*(4), 524–537. https://doi.org/10.1016/j.jretai.2014.05.004

Pancer, E., McShane, L., & Noseworthy, T. J. (2017). Isolated environmental cues and product efficacy penalties: The color green and eco-labels. *Journal of Business Ethics, 143*, 159–177. https://doi.org/10.1007/s10551-015-2764-4

Peukert, C., Pfeiffer, J., Meißner, M., Pfeiffer, T., & Weinhardt, C. (2019). Shopping in Virtual Reality stores: The influence of immersion on system adoption. *Journal of Management Information Systems, 36*(3), 755–788. https://doi.org/10.1080/07421222.2019.1628889

Pfeiffer, P., Pfeiffer, T., Meißner, M., & Weiß, E. (2020). Eye-Tracking-based classification of information search behavior using Machine Learning: Evidence from experiments in physical shops and Virtual Reality shopping environments. *Information Systems Research, 31*(3), 675–691. https://doi.org/10.1287/isre.2019.0907

Prakash, G., Choudhary, S., Kumar, A., Garza-Reyes, J. A., Khan, S. A. R., & Panda, T. K. (2019). Do altruistic and egoistic values influence consumers' attitudes and purchase intentions towards eco-friendly packaged products? An empirical investigation. *Journal of Retailing and Consumer Services, 50*, 163–169. https://doi.org/10.1016/j.jretconser.2019.05.011

Rees, W., Tremma, O., & Manning, L. (2019). Sustainability cues on packaging: The influence of recognition on purchasing behaviour. *Journal of Cleaner Production, 235*, 841–853. https://doi.org/10.1016/j.jclepro.2019.06.217

Rokka, J., & Uusitalo, L. (2008). Preference for green packaging in consumer product choices - do consumers care? *International Journal of Consumer Studies, 32*(5), 516–525. https://doi.org/10.1111/j.1470-6431.2008.00710.x

Samaraweera, M., Sims, J. D., & Homsey, D. M. (2021). Will a green color and nature images make consumers pay more for a green product? *Journal of Consumer Marketing, 38*(3), 305–312. https://doi.org/10.1108/JCM-04-2020-3771

Schnack, A., Wright, M. J., & Holdershaw, J. L. (2020). An exploratory investigation of shopper behaviour in an immersive virtual reality store. *Journal of Consumer Behaviour, 19*, 182–195. https://doi.org/10.1002/cb.1803

Scott, L., & Vigar-Ellis, D. (2014). Consumer understanding, perceptions and behaviours with regard to environmentally friendly packaging in a developing nation. *International Journal of Consumer Studies, 38*(6), 642–649. https://doi.org/10.1111/ijcs.12136

Seo, J., & Scammon, D. (2017). Do green packages lead to misperceptions? The influence of package colors on consumers' perceptions of brands with environmental claims. *Marketing Letters, 28*, 357–369. https://doi.org/10.1007/s11002-017-9420-y

Shimul, A. S., & Cheah, I. (2023). Consumers' preference for eco-friendly packaged products: Pride vs guilt appeal. *Marketing Intelligence & Planning, 41*(2), 186–198. https://doi.org/10.1108/MIP-05-2022-0197

Siegrist, M., Ung, C.-Y., Zank, M., Marinello, M., Kunz, A., Hartmann, C., & Menozzi, M. (2019). Consumers' food selection behaviors in three-dimensional (3D) virtual reality. *Food Research International, 117*, 50–59. https://doi.org/10.1016/j.foodres.2018.02.033

Singh, G., & Pandey, N. (2018). The determinants of green packaging that influence buyers' willingness to pay a price premium. *Australasian Marketing Journal, 26*(3), 221–230. https://doi.org/10.1016/j.ausmj.2018.06.001

Söderlund, M., Colliander, J., Karsberg, J., Liljedal, K. T., Modig, E., Rosengren, S., Sagfossen, S., Szugalski, S., & Åkestam, N. (2017). The allure of the bottle as a package: An assessment of perceived effort in a packaging context. *Journal of Product & Brand Management, 26*(1), 91–100. https://doi.org/10.1108/JPBM-12-2015-1065

Sprott, D. E., & Shimp, T. A. (2004). Using product sampling to augment the perceived quality of store brands. *Journal of Retailing, 80*(4), 305–315. https://doi.org/10.1016/j.jretai.2004.10.006

Steenis, N. D., van der Lans, I. A., van Herpen, E., & van Trijp, H. C. M. (2018). Effects of sustainable design strategies on consumer preferences for redesigned packaging. *Journal of Cleaner Production, 205*, 854–865. https://doi.org/10.1016/j.jclepro.2018.09.137

Steenis, N. D., van Herpen, E., van der Lans, I. A., Ligthart, T. N., & van Trijp, H. C. M. (2017). Consumer response to packaging design. The role of packaging materials and graphics in sustainability perceptions and product evaluations. *Journal of Cleaner Production, 162*, 286–298. https://doi.org/10.1016/j.jclepro.2017.06.036

Sundar, A., & Kellaris, J. J. (2017). How logo colors influence shoppers' judgments of retailer ethicality: The mediating role of perceived eco-friendliness. *Journal of Business Ethics, 146*, 685–701. https://doi.org/10.1007/s10551-015-2918-4

Trivedi, R. H., Patel, J. D., & Acharya, N. (2018). Causality analysis of media influence on environmental attitude, intention and behaviors leading to green purchasing. *Journal of Cleaner Production, 196*, 11–22. https://doi.org/10.1016/j.jclepro.2018.06.024

Tully, S. M., & Winer, R. S. (2014). The role of the beneficiary in willingness to pay for socially responsible products: A meta-analysis. *Journal of Retailing, 90*(2), 255–274. https://doi.org/10.1016/j.jretai.2014.03.004

Vecchio, R., & Annunziata, A. (2015). Willingness-to-pay for sustainability-labelled chocolate: An experimental auction approach. *Journal of Cleaner Production, 86*, 335–342. https://doi.org/10.1016/j.jclepro.2014.08.006

Wei, W., Kim, G., Miao, L., Behnke, C., & Almanza, B. (2018). Consumer inferences of Corporate Social Responsibility (CSR) claims on packaged foods. *Journal of Business Research, 83*, 186–201. https://doi.org/10.1016/j.jbusres.2017.10.046

Chapter 5
Preliminary Study and Main Experiments Procedure

5.1 Preliminary Study

The preliminary study was conducted before the main experiments through two focus groups. The goal was to check if:

(a) the packaging manipulations were perceived by the individuals as planned during the research design phase (Gosselt et al., 2019);
(b) the proposed stimuli were relevant to individuals (Gosselt et al., 2019);
(c) a realistic stimulus appearance was achieved, with mock-ups designed similar to the products commonly available on the market;
(d) there was room for improvement in clarity or errors in the designed stimuli; and
(e) to have preliminary feedback on the direction of the research hypotheses.

Two online focus groups were conducted, each involving eight participants, for a total of sixteen individuals (see Table 5.1 for sample details; Branca et al., 2023). Participants were recruited using convenience and snowball sampling. After providing informed consent, they were invited to join one of the two sessions.

Both focus groups followed the same procedure and employed identical stimuli (Millward, 2012; Wilkinson, 2008). At the start of each session, participants were welcomed and thanked, and a brief introduction was read outlining the session's purpose, structure, and focus on packaging alternatives and sustainability. Participants were informed that audio recordings would be made to support content analysis.

The three packaging manipulations, namely structural, haptic, and visual cues, were presented sequentially. For each set, the moderator asked participants to identify the most eco-friendly alternative and explain their reasoning, encouraging discussion and interaction. The sessions were transcribed, supplemented with observational notes, and subsequently analyzed.

Although the stimuli were presented on screen, participants clearly perceived the manipulations as intended, recognizing the differences between them and finding the

G. Branca, *Virtual Reality, Real Intentions*, International Series in Advanced Management Studies, https://doi.org/10.1007/978-3-032-10142-6_5

Table 5.1 Demographics of the preliminary study

		Focus group 1	Focus group 2
Gender	Male Female	4 (50%) 4 (50%)	4 (50%) 4 (50%)
Age	Range Mean	21–51 34.63	21–59 35.87
Education level	Less than high school High school diploma Specialized/Vocational/Technical training Bachelor's degree Master's degree Doctoral Degree	- (-) 4 (50%) - (-) 1 (12,5%) 2 (25%) 1 (12.5%)	1 (12.5%) 3 (37.5%) - (-) 2 (25%) 1 (12.5%) 1 (12.5%)
Occupation	Employed Self-employed/Freelance Homemaker Student Other	3 (37.5%) 1 (12.5%) 1 (12.5%) 2 (25%) 1 (12.5%)	2 (25%) 2 (25%) 1 (12.5%) 2 (25%) 1 (12.5%)

Source Branca et al. (2023)

stimuli relevant. However, some minor refinements were necessary to enhance their quality. The shape of the cardboard packaging was slightly adjusted for greater visual appeal, the visual design was reworked to achieve a more balanced composition, and a pastel color palette was adopted to increase realism and coherence across the mock-ups.

5.2 Main Experiment Procedure

5.2.1 *Pilot Test and Manipulation Check*

Before running the main experiment, a pilot test was conducted, to verify the research protocol (in line with Naderi et al., 2020) and for the manipulation check. The procedure worked as planned, and there was no evidence of issues related to the experimental procedure, timing, measurements, questionnaires, and technologies employed. Eighteen participants were involved (age range 18–34) and thus excluded from the main experiment. They were assigned randomly either to the VR condition (55.56% females) or the PR condition (55.56% males).

In the pilot test an additional question, not included in the main experiment questionnaire, was used for the manipulation check. For the structural manipulations, the participants were asked to indicate the packaging materials. All participants in VR and PR indicated the material as intended by the research design. For the visual manipulations, subjects were asked to indicate what the colors of the packaging were. In both conditions, all subjects indicated the colors as intended by the research design.

Finally, for the haptic manipulations, participants were asked to evaluate the cardboard surface on a 4-item 7-point semantic differential scale ("This milk pack is": 1 = matte/7 = shiny; 1 = not reflective/7 = reflective; 1 = unrefined/7 = polished; 1 = rough/7 = smooth). While for the PR condition, results of the ANOVA showed a significant effect of haptic manipulation ($M_{baseline} = 4.19$; $M_{rough} = 1.75$; $M_{smooth} = 5.64$), for the VR condition there was not a significant effect ($M_{baseline} = 4.5$; $M_{rough} = 4.08$; $M_{smooth} = 4.72$). Building on this result, some minor adjustments were provided in the VR packaging, making the differences among the textures more noticeable.

A new manipulation check was conducted during the main study, only for the haptic cues group in the VR condition, since the other manipulation checks confirmed the effectiveness of our design. 20 random participants were asked to rate the packaging, similar to what was done previously. In this case, the result of the ANOVA showed a significant effect of haptic manipulation ($M_{baseline} = 4.64$; $M_{rough} = 3.13$; $M_{smooth} = 5.36$).

5.2.2 *Main Experiments Procedure and Participants*

A convenience sample of 167 Italian consumers participated in the main experiment in a university laboratory setting in Benevento (Italy). They were randomly assigned either to the VR (82, 51.2% males) or the PR (83, 53.0% males) condition, and compensated by drawing five Amazon 30 euros gift cards. Subjects were required to complete the tasks either in VR or in PR (see Table 5.2 for sample details; Branca et al., 2023).

Participants were informed that the purpose of the research was to evaluate some milk packs not yet available on the market, thus encouraging them to examine the product as long as they desired (Kang et al., 2020). To avoid preference bias due to packaging position, packaging was shown one by one, in a random order. The presentation contexts can play a role in consumer response to packaging design (Machiels & Orth, 2017; Orth & Crouch, 2014). After each packaging evaluation, participants were required to complete a self-report questionnaire containing the dependent variables and, at the end of the experiment, to provide demographic information.

In the VR condition, a high-immersive Head Mounted Display (Oculus Quest 2) was employed, combined with a Leap Motion Controller for hand tracking. This technology allows users to freely use their hands without the need for controllers, improving the realism of the experience, ensuring accuracy and near-zero latency. Furthermore, the VR environment provided a realistic simulation of light behavior with ray tracing technology. For this purpose, two light sources (i.e., two windows), were provided in the virtual room. Before participating in the main task, namely packaging evaluations, participants took part in a training session in the same VR room: using an orange cubic item (shown in Fig. 5.1), not included in the stimuli, they

Table 5.2 Demographics of the main experiments

		VR	PR
Gender	Male	43 (51.2%)	44 (53.0%)
	Female	41 (48.8%)	39 (47.0%)
Age	18–24	33 (39.3%)	34 (41.0%)
	25–34	36 (42.9%)	36 (36.4%)
	35–44	2 (2.4%)	2 (2.4%)
	45–54	6 (7.1%)	4 (4.8%)
	55–64	7 (8.3%)	7 (8.4%)
Education level	Less than high school	2 (2.4%)	3 (3.6%)
	High school diploma	34 (40.5%)	34 (41.0%)
	Specialized/Vocational/Technical training	1 (1.2%)	1 (1.2%)
	Bachelor's degree	18 (21.4%)	21 (25.3%)
	Master's degree	21 (25.0%)	22 (26.5%)
	Doctoral Degree	8 (9.5%)	2 (2.4%)
Occupation	Employed	19 (22.6%)	17 (20.5%)
	Self-employed/Freelance	8 (9.5%)	13 (15.7%)
	Unemployed - Looking for work	2 (2.4%)	6 (7.2%)
	Unemployed - Not looking for work	1 (1.2%)	1 (1.2%)
	Homemaker	1 (1.2%)	2 (2.4%)
	Student	41 (48.8%)	38 (45.8%)
	Retired	- (-)	1 (1.2%)
	Other	12 (14.3%)	5 (6.0%)

Source Branca et al. (2023)

had the chance to become familiar with the environment and the VR experience. In the virtual environment, participants were free to move in any direction, look around, approach objects, grab the packages with one or both hands (with a natural gesture), rotate their wrists, move around the packaging, and deposit it anywhere in the room. Figure 5.2 shows some participants during the task in VR.

In PR, as in VR, participants viewed one packaging at a time, in a random order, in a neutral room.

5.3 Main Experiments Overview

The following three chapters present the empirical core of this research. Chapter 6 reports Study 1, which investigates structural cues in VR vs. PR, building on and extending Branca et al. (2023). Chapter 7 reports Study 2, which focuses on haptic

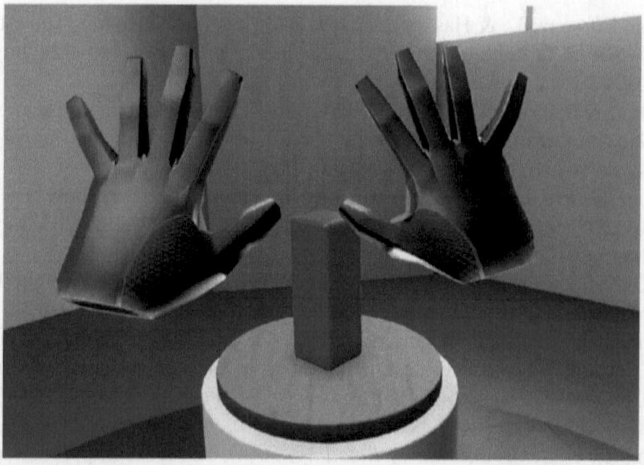

Fig. 5.1 The object used for the VR training task (Branca et al., 2023)

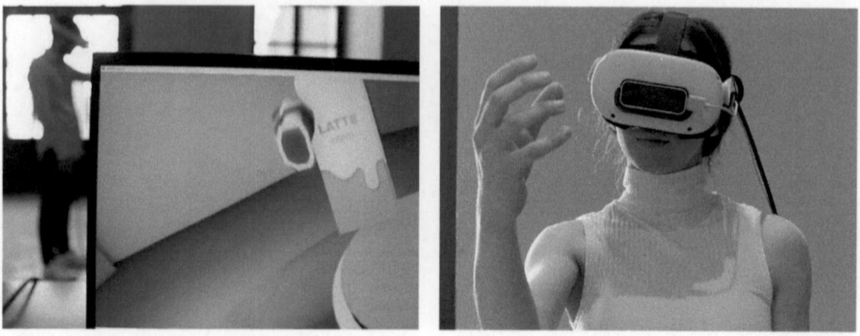

Fig. 5.2 Participants during the task in VR

cues, building on and extending Branca et al. (2023). Finally, Chap. 8 reports Study 3, considering visual cues.

For each of the three studies, a mixed Analysis of Variance (ANOVA) was conducted, which means repeated measures within-subject ANOVA (i.e., packaging manipulations) with a between-subject factor (i.e., VR vs PR). IBM SPSS Statistic, version 28.0, was used for the analysis.

References

Branca, G., Resciniti, R., & Loureiro, S. M. C. (2023). Virtual is so real! Consumers' evaluation of product packaging in virtual reality. *Psychology & Marketing, 40*, 596–609. https://doi.org/10.1002/mar.21743

Gosselt, J. F., van Rompay, T., & Haske, L. (2019). Won't get fooled again: The effects of internal and external CSR ECO-Labeling. *Journal of Business Ethics, 155*, 413–424. https://doi.org/10.1007/s10551-017-3512-8

Kang, H. J., Shin, J., & Ponto, K. (2020). How 3D Virtual Reality stores can shape consumer purchase decisions: The roles of informativeness and playfulness. *Journal of Interactive Marketing, 49*, 70–85. https://doi.org/10.1016/j.intmar.2019.07.002

Machiels, C. J. A., & Orth, U. R. (2017). Verticality in product labels and shelves as a metaphorical cue to quality. *Journal of Retailing and Consumer Services, 37*, 195–203. https://doi.org/10.1016/j.jretconser.2017.02.009

Millward, L. (2012). Focus groups. In G. M. Breakwell, J. A. Smith, & D. B. Wright (Eds.), *Research Methods in Psychology* (4th ed.). Sage.

Naderi, E., Naderi, I., & Balakrishnan, B. (2020). Product design matters, but is it enough? Consumers' responses to product design and environment congruence. *Journal of Product & Brand Management, 29*(7), 939–954. https://doi.org/10.1108/JPBM-08-2018-1975

Orth, U. R., & Crouch, R. C. (2014). Is beauty in the aisles of the retailer? Package processing in visually complex contexts. *Journal of Retailing, 90*(4), 524–537. https://doi.org/10.1016/j.jretai.2014.05.004

Wilkinson, S. (2008). Focus groups. In G. M. Breakwell (Ed.), *Doing Social Psychology Research.* Wiley-Blackwell.

Chapter 6
Study 1—Consumers' Response to Structural Cues

6.1 Study 1 Results

6.1.1 Perceived Sustainability

The plastic bottle is perceived as the least sustainable solution in both treatments (VR: $M_{VRplastic} = 2.9$, $SD_{VRplastic} = 1.68$; PR: $M_{PRplastic} = 2.52$, $SD_{PRplastic} = 1.53$). The glass bottle was perceived as a more sustainable alternative in both treatments (VR: $M_{VRglass} = 5.1$, $SD_{VRglass} = 1.79$; PR: $M_{PRglass} = 5.83$, $SD_{PRglass} = 1.47$) followed by the baseline carton packaging (VR: $M_{VRbaseline} = 4.6$, $SD_{VRbaseline} = 1.63$; PR: $M_{PRbaseline} = 4.68$, $SD_{PRbaseline} = 1.62$). Thus, H-PS1 is supported in both conditions.

Levene's Test of Equality of Error Variances shows *p*-values of more than 0.05 (0.272, 0.607, 0.052). Mauchly's Test of Sphericity shows a *p*-value more than 0.05 (0.344). Looking at the Multivariate Tests, there is evidence of a significant main effect since the *p*-values are less than 0.05. The Tests of Within-Subjects Contrasts show a significant linear effect since the *p*-value is less than 0.05 (<0.001). The Between-Subjects Effect was found to be not significant ($F(1,165) = 0.701$, $p = 0.404$). There was not a significant difference in between-groups for the plastic bottle and the baseline manipulation, since the *p*-values are more than 0.05 (0.128, 0.753), while a significant difference was found between the two conditions for the glass bottle ($p = 0.004$). Thus, H1 is partially supported for the structural manipulations. A significant difference in the within-subjects groups is found for all the manipulations, except for the baseline carton and the glass bottle in VR condition ($p = 0.073$).

Figure 6.1 presents the means and standard deviations results.

G. Branca, *Virtual Reality, Real Intentions*, International Series in Advanced Management Studies, https://doi.org/10.1007/978-3-032-10142-6_6

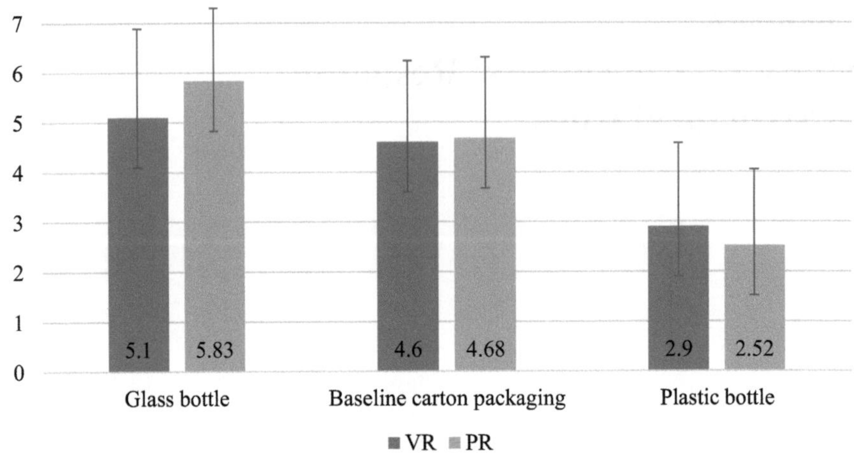

Fig. 6.1 Structural cues, perceived sustainability

6.1.2 *Willingness to Pay a Premium Price*

The glass bottle is the option with the highest WTPP across both treatments (VR: $M_{VRglass} = 4.87$, $SD_{VRglass} = 1.73$; PR: $M_{PRglass} = 5.32$, $SD_{PRglass} = 1.65$), followed by the baseline carton packaging (VR: $M_{VRbaseline} = 3.74$, $SD_{VRbaseline} = 1.58$; PR: $M_{PRbaseline} = 3.95$, $SD_{PRbaseline} = 1.6$) and the plastic bottle (VR: $M_{VRplastic} = 2.57$, $SD_{VRplastic} = 1.56$; PR: $M_{PRplastic} = 2.51$, $SD_{PRplastic} = 1.45$). Thus, H-WTPP1 is supported in both conditions.

Levene's Test of Equality of Error Variances shows *p*-values more than 0.05 (0.657, 0.775, 0.607). Mauchly's Test of Sphericity shows a *p*-value more than 0.05 (0.908). Looking at the Multivariate Tests, there is evidence of a significant main effect, since the *p*-values are less than 0.05. The Tests of Within-Subjects Contrasts show a significant linear effect since the *p*-value is less than 0.05 (<0.001). The Between-Subject Effect is not significant ($F(1,165) = 1.399$, $p = 0.239$). There was not a significant difference in between-groups means, since the *p*-values are more than 0.05 (0.799, 0.386, 0.088). Thus, H2 is supported for the structural manipulations. A significant difference in the within-subjects groups is found for all the manipulations since the *p*-values are less than 0.05.

Figure 6.2 presents the means and standard deviations results.

6.1.3 *Purchase Intention*

The glass bottle scored similar PI in VR ($M_{VRglass} = 4.86$, $SD_{VRglass} = 1.62$) and in PR ($M_{PRglass} = 5.28$, $SD_{PRglass} = 1.57$). The baseline carton packaging elicited similar PI in VR ($M_{VRbaseline} = 4.10$, $SD_{VRbaseline} = 1.52$) and PR ($M_{PRbaseline} = 4.14$,

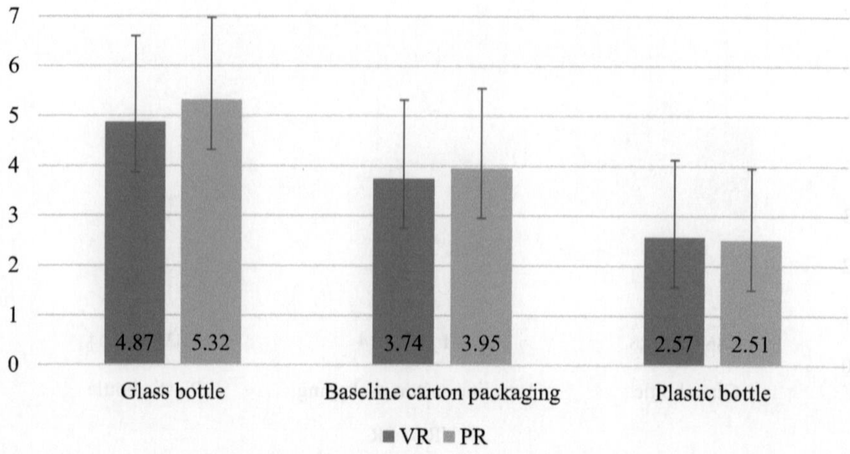

Fig. 6.2 Structural cues, willingness to pay a premium price

$SD_{PRbaseline} = 1.45$). The same happened for the plastic bottle in VR ($M_{VRplastic} = 3.33$, $SD_{VRplastic} = 1.53$) and PR ($M_{PRplastic} = 3.04$, $SD_{PRplastic} = 1.37$). Thus, PI1 is supported in both conditions.

Levene's Test of Equality of Error Variances shows *p*-values more than 0.05 (0.208, 0.407, 0.861). Mauchly's Test of Sphericity shows a *p*-value less than 0.05 (0.011). The Greenhouse–Geisser corrected analysis and the Huynh–Feldt ($p < 0.001$) in the Tests of Within-Subjects Effects are less than 0.05, while the interaction is slightly more than 0.05 (0.057). The Tests of Within-Subjects Contrasts show a significant linear effect since the *p*-value is less than 0.05 (<0.001). The Between-Subject Effects are not significant ($F(1,165) = 0.122$, $p = 0.727$). There is not a significant difference in between-groups means, since the *p*-values are more than 0.05 (0.189, 0.871, 0.086). Thus, H3 is supported for the structural manipulations. A significant difference in the within-subjects groups is found for all the manipulations since the *p*-values are less than 0.05.

Figure 6.3 presents the means and standard deviations results.

6.1.4 Attitude Toward Packaging

The glass bottle scored similar ATP in VR ($M_{VRglass} = 5.27$, $SD_{VRglass} = 1.52$) and in PR ($M_{PRglass} = 5.80$, $SD_{PRglass} = 1.47$). The baseline carton packaging elicited similar ATP results in VR ($M_{VRbaseline} = 4.42$, $SD_{VRbaseline} = 1.58$) and in PR ($M_{PRbaseline} = 4.61$, $SD_{PRbaseline} = 1.43$). The same happened for the plastic bottle in VR ($M_{VRplastic} = 3.58$, $SD_{VRplastic} = 1.66$) and in PR ($M_{PRplastic} = 3.16$, $SD_{PRplastic} = 1.43$). Thus, H-ATP1 is supported in both conditions.

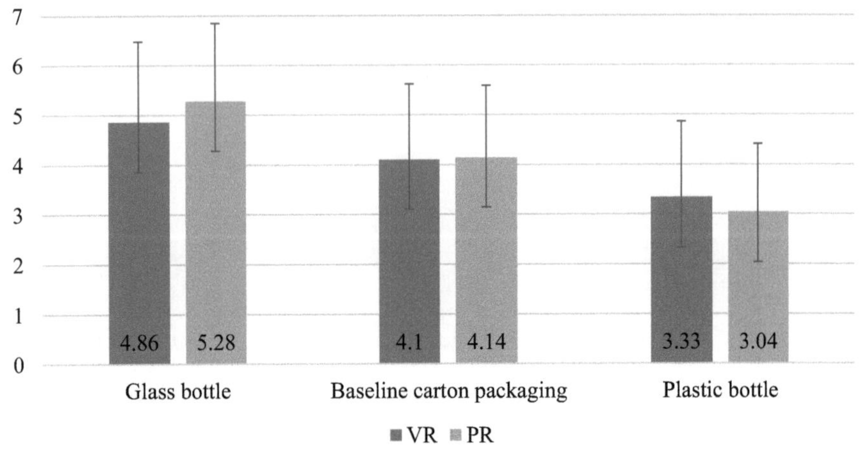

Fig. 6.3 Structural cues, purchase intention

Levene's Test of Equality of Error Variances shows *p*-values more than 0.05 for the plastic bottle (0.127) and the glass one (0.368), while the baseline is slightly lower than 0.05 (0.042). Mauchly's Test of Sphericity shows a *p*-value more than 0.05 (0.051). Looking at the Multivariate Tests, there is evidence of a significant main effect, since the *p*-values are less than 0.05. The Tests of Within-Subjects Contrast shows a significant linear effect since the *p*-value is less than 0.05 (<0.001). The Between-Subject Effects are not significant ($F\ (1,165) = 0.378$, $p = 0.539$). There is not a significant difference in between-groups for the plastic bottle and the baseline manipulation, since the *p*-values are more than 0.05 (0.077, 0397), while a significant difference is found between the two conditions for the glass bottle ($p = 0.026$). Thus, H4 is partially supported for the structural manipulations. A significant difference in the within-subjects groups is found for all the manipulations since the *p*-values are less than 0.05.

Figure 6.4 presents the means and standard deviations results.

6.1.5 Perceived Quality

The glass bottle scored similar PQ in VR ($M_{VRglass} = 5.60$, $SD_{VRglass} = 1.33$) and in PR ($M_{PRglass} = 5.78$, $SD_{PRglass} = 1.20$). The baseline carton packaging elicited similar PQ in VR ($M_{VRbaseline} = 4.46$, $SD_{VRbaseline} = 1.48$) and PR ($M_{PRbaseline} = 4.55$, $SD_{PRbaseline} = 1.46$). The same happened for the plastic bottle in VR ($M_{VRplastic} = 3.91$, $SD_{VRplastic} = 1.64$) and PR ($M_{PRplastic} = 3.67$, $SD_{PRplastic} = 1.48$). Thus, H-PQ1 is supported in both conditions.

Levene's Test of Equality of Error Variances shows *p*-values more than 0.05 (0.449, 0.623, 0.535). Mauchly's Test of Sphericity shows a *p*-value of more than

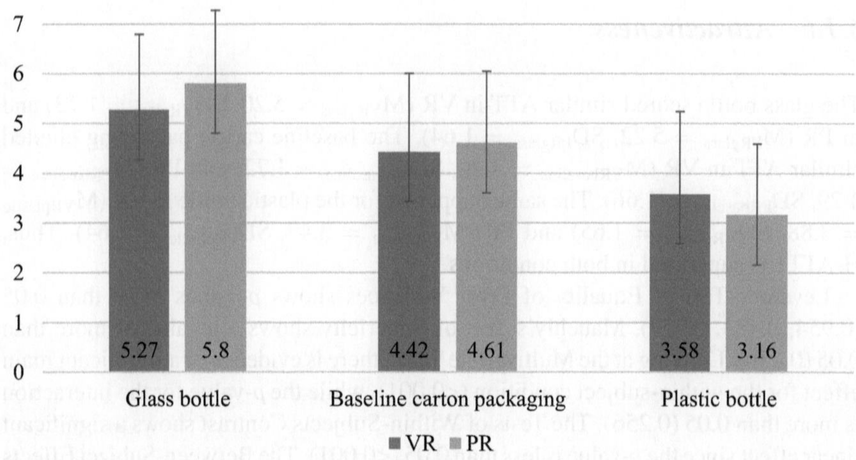

Fig. 6.4 Structural cues, attitude toward packaging

0.05 (0.067). Looking at the Multivariate Tests, there is evidence of a significant main effect for the within-subject condition (<0.001), while the *p*-value for the interaction is more than 0.05 (0.309). The Tests of Within-Subjects Contrasts show a significant linear effect since the *p*-value is less than 0.05 (<0.001). The Between-Subject Effects are not significant (F (1,165) = 0.006, *p* = 0.940). There is not a significant difference in between-groups means, since the *p*-values are more than 0.05 (0.320, 0.693, 0.339). Thus, H5 is supported for the structural manipulations. A significant difference in the within-subjects groups is found for all the manipulations since the *p*-values are less than 0.05.

Figure 6.5 presents the means and standard deviations results.

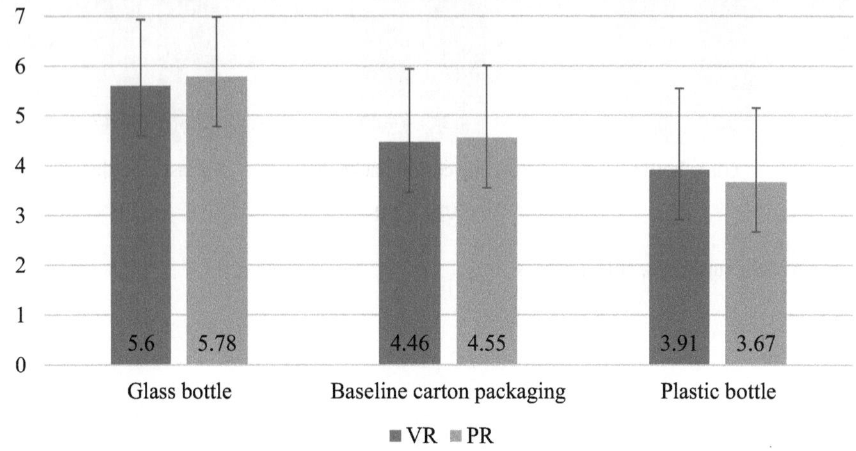

Fig. 6.5 Structural cues, perceived quality

6.1.6 Attractiveness

The glass bottle scored similar ATT in VR ($M_{VRglass} = 5.20$, $SD_{VRglass} = 1.73$) and in PR ($M_{PRglass} = 5.22$, $SD_{PRglass} = 1.64$). The baseline carton packaging elicited similar ATT in VR ($M_{VRbaseline} = 4.20$, $SD_{VRbaseline} = 1.72$) and PR ($M_{PRbaseline} = 4.29$, $SD_{PRbaseline} = 1.66$). The same happened for the plastic bottle in VR ($M_{VRplastic} = 3.88$, $SD_{VRplastic} = 1.65$) and PR ($M_{PRplastic} = 3.47$, $SD_{PRplastic} = 1.64$). Thus, H-ATT1 is supported in both conditions.

Levene's Test of Equality of Error Variances shows p-values more than 0.05 (0.954, 0.483, 0.777). Mauchly's Test of Sphericity shows a p-value of more than 0.05 (0.270). Looking at the Multivariate Tests, there is evidence of a significant main effect for the within-subject condition (<0.001), while the p-value for the interaction is more than 0.05 (0.256). The Tests of Within-Subjects Contrast shows a significant linear effect since the p-value is less than 0.05 (<0.001). The Between-Subject Effects are not significant ($F(1,165) = 0.349, p = 0.556$). There is not a significant difference in between-groups means, since the p-values are more than 0.05 (0.108, 0.740, 0.956). Thus, H6 is supported for the structural manipulations. A significant difference in the within-subjects groups is found for all the manipulations since the p-values are less than 0.05, except for the plastic bottle and the baseline packaging in VR.

Figure 6.6 presents the means and standard deviations results.

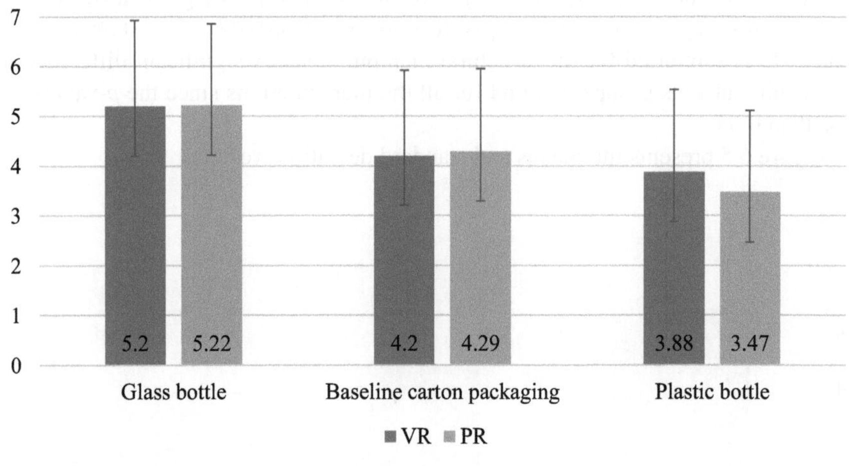

Fig. 6.6 Structural cues, attractiveness

6.2 Discussion

Some main discussion points emerge from the analysis of structural packaging cues (glass bottle, carton pack, plastic bottle) across VR and PR, extending Branca et al. (2023).

First, the results indicate largely consistent consumer evaluations across VR and PR, with mostly no statistical differences across all the comparisons and variables. While minor statistical differences were observed, namely PS and ATP of the glass bottle, the overall preference pattern remained stable.

Second, examining the single manipulations across VR and PR, some differences in magnitude emerged. Notably, the glass bottle frequently scored higher in PR than VR for several dependent variables, possibly due to the difficulty of simulating tactile or weight-based cues in VR. Conversely, the plastic bottle consistently scored slightly higher in VR than PR, possibly due to reduced diagnosticity that downplays its typical negative associations. However, even if the level of responses may vary, the preference structure remained stable, supporting the suitability of VR for comparative evaluations, while hinting at a less polarized evaluation in virtual settings.

Third, in terms of within-packaging manipulation comparisons, the pattern among material types was supported. Consumers showed a strong preference for the glass bottle. Plastic, by contrast, was clearly seen as the least desirable across all attitudinal dimensions. These findings also strengthen the link between PS and other attitudinal measures for packaging material: when it comes to structural cues, if the packaging is perceived as more sustainable, it elicits a more positive attitudinal response.

References

Branca, G., Resciniti, R., & Loureiro, S. M. C. (2023). Virtual is so real! Consumers' evaluation of product packaging in virtual reality. *Psychology & Marketing, 40*, 596–609. https://doi.org/10.1002/mar.21743

Chapter 7
Study 2—Consumers' Response to Haptic Cues

7.1 Study 2 Results

7.1.1 Perceived Sustainability

The smooth packaging is perceived as the less sustainable solution, especially in the PR condition (VR: $M_{VRsmooth} = 4.35$, $SD_{VRsmooth} = 1.78$; PR: $M_{PRsmooth} = 3.78$, $SD_{PRsmooth} = 1.81$). The rough pack is perceived as the most sustainable alternative in the group, across both treatments (VR: $M_{VRrough} = 5.24$, $SD_{VRrough} = 1.42$; PR: $M_{PRrough} = 5.42$, $SD_{PRrough} = 1.58$), followed by the baseline carton packaging (VR: $M_{VRbaseline} = 4.6$, $SD_{VRbaseline} = 1.63$; PR: $M_{PRbaseline} = 4.68$, $SD_{PRbaseline} = 1.62$). Thus, H-PS2 is supported in both conditions.

Levene's Test of Equality of Error Variances shows *p*-values more than 0.05 (0.171, 0.607, 0.839). Mauchly's Test of Sphericity shows a *p*-value less than 0.05 ($p > 0.001$). Interpreting the Greenhouse-Geisser corrected analysis ($p = < 0.001$) and the Huynh-Feldt correction ($p = 0.004$) in the Tests of Within-Subjects Effects, we have evidence of a significant main effect, because the *p*-values are less than 0.05. The Tests of Within-Subjects Contrasts show a significant linear effect since the *p*-value is less than 0.05 (<0.001). The Between-Subject Effect is found to be not significant ($F(1,165) = 0.234$, $p = 0.629$). There is not a significant difference in between-groups for the rough and the baseline manipulation, since the *p*-values are more than 0.05 (0.461, 0.753), while a significant difference is found between the two conditions for the smooth bottle ($p = 0.043$). Thus, H1 is partially supported for the haptic manipulations. A significant difference in the within-subjects groups is found for all the manipulations, except for the baseline carton and the smooth one in VR ($p = 0.341$).

Figure 7.1 presents the means and standard deviations results.

G. Branca, *Virtual Reality, Real Intentions*, International Series in Advanced Management Studies, https://doi.org/10.1007/978-3-032-10142-6_7

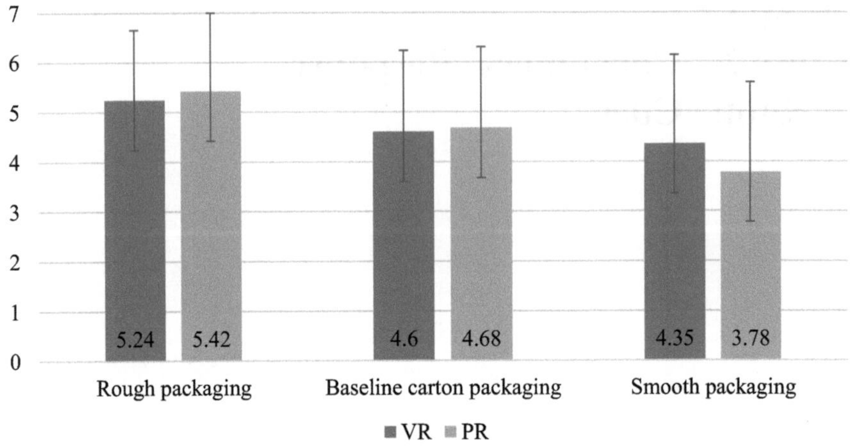

Fig. 7.1 Haptic cues, perceived sustainability

7.1.2 Willingness to Pay a Premium Price

The rough packaging is the alternative with the highest WTPP across both treatments (VR: $M_{VRrough} = 4.38$, $SD_{VRrough} = 1.53$; PR: $M_{PRrough} = 4.5$, $SD_{PRrough} = 1.65$), followed by the baseline carton in PR condition (PR: $M_{PRbaseline} = 3.95$, $SD_{PRbaseline} = 1.6$; PR: $M_{PRsmooth} = 3.33$, $SD_{PRsmooth} = 1.63$) and by the smooth packaging in VR condition (VR: $M_{VRsmooth} = 3.77$, $SD_{VRsmooth} = 1.73$; VR: $M_{VRbaseline} = 3.74$, $SD_{VRbaseline} = 1.58$). However, H-WTPP2 is partially supported for the VR condition and supported for the PR condition.

Levene's Test of Equality of Error Variances shows *p*-values more than 0.05 (0.481, 0.775, 0.552). Mauchly's Test of Sphericity shows a *p*-value less than 0.05 ($p < 0.001$). Interpreting the Greenhouse–Geisser corrected analysis ($p < 0.001$) and the Huynh-Feldt correction ($p = 0.007$) in the Tests of Within-Subjects Effects, we have evidence of a significant main effect, because the *p*-values are less than 0.05. The Tests of Within-Subjects Contrasts show a significant linear effect since the *p*-value is less than 0.05 (<0.001). The Between-Subject Effect is found to be not significant ($F(1,165) = 0.032$, $p = 0.859$). There is not a significant difference in between-groups means, since all the *p*-values are more than 0.05 (0.630, 0.386, 0.086). Thus, H2 is supported for the haptic manipulations. A significant difference in the within-subjects groups is found for all the manipulations, since the *p*-values are less than 0.05, except for the baseline carton and the smooth one in the VR condition ($p = 1.000$).

Figure 7.2 presents the means and standard deviations results.

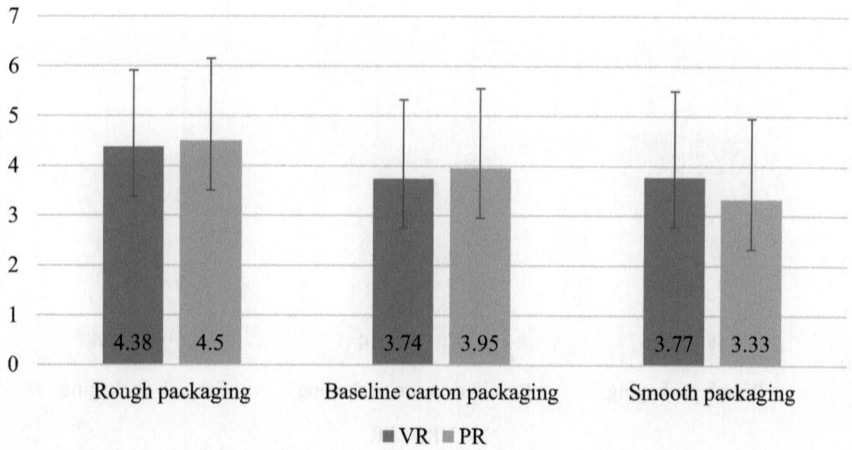

Fig. 7.2 Haptic cues, willingness to pay a premium price

7.1.3 Purchase Intention

The rough packaging scores a similar PI in VR ($M_{VRrough} = 4.58$, $SD_{VRrough} = 1.43$) and in PR ($M_{PRrough} = 4.67$, $SD_{PRrough} = 1.54$). The baseline carton packaging elicited similar PI results in VR ($M_{VRbaseline} = 4.10$, $SD_{VRbaseline} = 1.52$) and in PR ($M_{PRbaseline} = 4.14$, $SD_{PRbaseline} = 1.45$). The same happened with the smooth packaging in VR ($M_{VRsmooth} = 4.19$, $SD_{VRsmooth} = 1.53$) and in PR ($M_{PRsmooth} = 3.98$, $SD_{PRsmooth} = 1.58$). In this case also, H-PI2 is partially supported for the VR condition and supported for the PR condition.

Levene's Test of Equality of Error Variances shows *p*-values more than 0.05 (0.376, 0.407, 0.468). Mauchly's Test of Sphericity shows a *p*-value less than 0.05 (>0.001). The Greenhouse–Geisser corrected analysis and the Huynh–Feldt ($p = <0.001$) in the Tests of Within-Subjects Effects are less than 0.05, while the interaction is more than 0.05 (0.313). The Tests of Within-Subjects Contrasts show a significant linear effect since the *p*-value is less than 0.05 (<0.001). The Between-Subject Effects are found to be not significant ($F(1,165) = 0.018, p = 0.894$). There is not a significant difference in between-groups means, since the *p*-values are more than 0.05 (0.691, 0.871, 0.388). Thus, H3 is supported for the haptic manipulations. A significant difference in the within-subjects groups is found only for the rough packaging and the baseline in VR (0.002), and for the rough packaging with the baseline and with the smooth one in PR (<0.001), while the other pairwise comparisons were found not significant.

Figure 7.3 presents the means and standard deviations results.

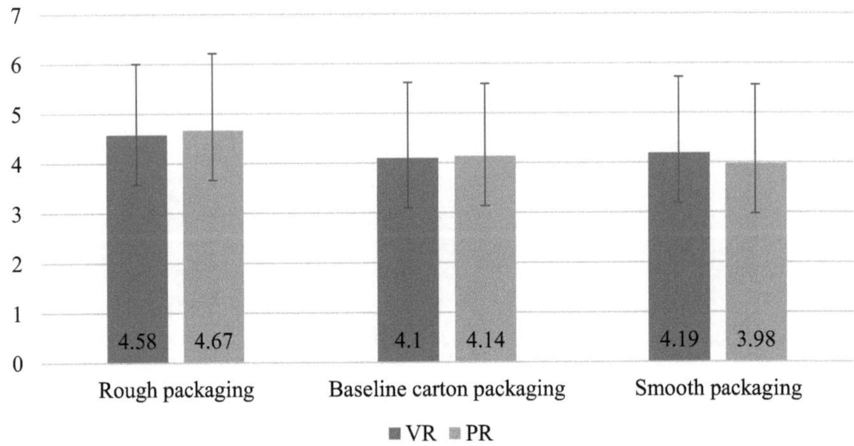

Fig. 7.3 Haptic cues, purchase intention

7.1.4 Attitude Toward Packaging

The rough packaging shows the highest ATP in VR ($M_{VRrough} = 4.85$, $SD_{VRrough} = 1.37$) and in PR ($M_{PRrough} = 5.06$, $SD_{PRrough} = 1.47$). The baseline packaging elicited similar ATP in VR ($M_{VRbaseline} = 4.42$, $SD_{VRbaseline} = 1.58$) and in PR ($M_{PRbaseline} = 4.61$, $SD_{PRbaseline} = 1.43$). The same happened with the smooth packaging in VR ($M_{VRsmooth} = 4.50$, $SD_{VRsmooth} = 1.55$) and in PR ($M_{PRsmooth} = 3.85$, $SD_{PRsmooth} = 1.59$). However, H-ATP2 is partially supported for the VR condition and supported for the PR condition.

Levene's Test of Equality of Error Variances shows *p*-values more than 0.05 for the rough packaging (0.646) and the smooth one (0.921), while the baseline one is slightly lower than 0.05 (0.042). Mauchly's Test of Sphericity shows a *p*-value less than 0.05 (0.014). Interpreting the Greenhouse–Geisser corrected analysis and the Huynh–Feldt ($p = < 0.001$) in the Tests of Within-Subjects Effects, there is evidence of a significant main effect because the *p*-values are less than 0.05. The Tests of Within-Subjects Contrasts show a significant linear effect since the *p*-value is less than 0.05 (<0.001). The Between-Subject Effects are found to be not significant ($F(1,165) = 0.161$, $p = 0.689$). There is not a significant difference in between-groups means for rough and baseline packaging, since the *p*-values are more than 0.05 (0.329, 0.397), except for the smooth packaging (0.009). Thus, H4 is partially supported for the haptic manipulations. A significant difference in the within-subjects groups is found for the rough and the baseline packaging in VR (0.013) and all the manipulations in PR, while the remaining pairwise comparisons were found not significant.

Figure 7.4 presents the means and standard deviations results.

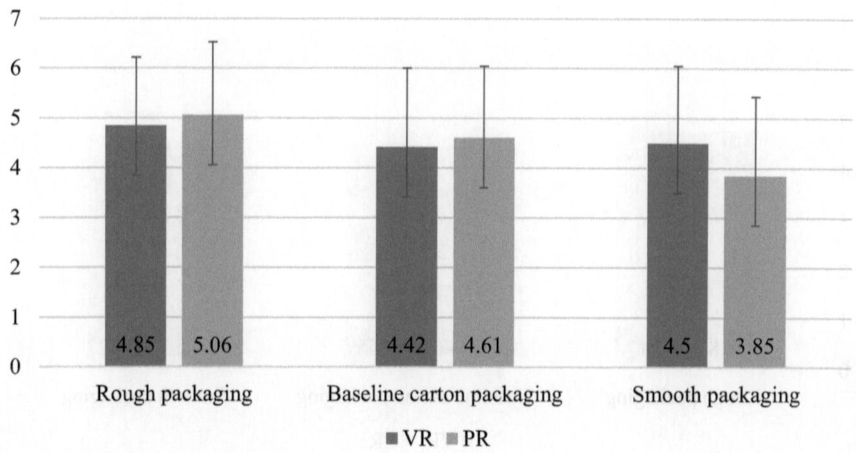

Fig. 7.4 Haptic cues, attitude toward packaging

7.1.5 Perceived Quality

The rough packaging shows a similar PQ result in VR ($M_{VRrough} = 4.80$, $SD_{VRrough} = 1.42$) and in PR ($M_{PRrough} = 5.17$, $SD_{PRrough} = 1.35$). The baseline carton packaging elicited similar PQ results in VR ($M_{VRbaseline} = 4.46$, $SD_{VRbaseline} = 1.48$) and in PR ($M_{PRbaseline} = 4.55$, $SD_{PRbaseline} = 1.46$). The same happened with the smooth packaging in VR ($M_{VRsmooth} = 4.55$, $SD_{VRsmooth} = 1.40$) and in PR ($M_{PRsmooth} = 4.27$, $SD_{PRsmooth} = 1.41$). However, H-PQ2 is partially supported for the VR condition and supported for the PR condition.

Levene's Test of Equality of Error Variances shows *p*-values more than 0.05 (0.490, 0.623, 0.788). Mauchly's Test of Sphericity shows a *p*-value of more than 0.05 (0.153). Looking at the Multivariate Tests, there is evidence of a significant main effect since the *p*-values are less than 0.05. The Tests of Within-Subjects Contrast shows a significant linear effect since the *p*-value is less than 0.05 (<0.001). The Between-Subject Effects are not significant ($F(1,165) = 0.443$, $p = 0.749$). There is not a significant difference in between-groups means, since the *p*-values are more than 0.05 (0.086, 0.693, 0.196). Thus, H5 is supported for the haptic manipulations. A significant difference in the within-subjects groups is found only for the rough packaging with the baseline and the smooth packaging in PR (<0.001), while the other pairwise comparisons were found not significant.

Figure 7.5 presents the means and standard deviations results.

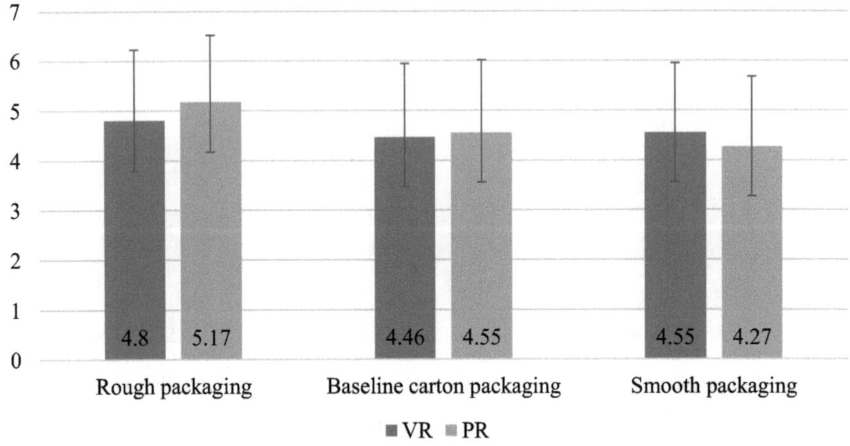

Fig. 7.5 Haptic cues, perceived quality

7.1.6 Attractiveness

The rough packaging shows a similar ATT result in VR ($M_{VRrough} = 4.55$, $SD_{VRrough} = 1.50$) and in PR ($M_{PRrough} = 4.88$, $SD_{PRrough} = 1.65$). The baseline carton packaging elicited similar ATT results in VR ($M_{VRbaseline} = 4.20$, $SD_{VRbaseline} = 1.72$) and in PR ($M_{PRbaseline} = 4.29$, $SD_{PRbaseline} = 1.66$). The same happened with the smooth packaging in VR ($M_{VRsmooth} = 4.36$, $SD_{VRsmooth} = 1.63$) and in PR ($M_{PRsmooth} = 4.12$, $SD_{PRsmooth} = 1.64$). In this case also, H-ATT2 is partially supported for the VR condition and supported for the PR condition.

Levene's Test of Equality of Error Variances shows *p*-values more than 0.05 (0.302, 0.483, 0.480). Mauchly's Test of Sphericity shows a *p*-value of more than 0.05 (0.138). Looking at the Multivariate Tests, there is evidence of a significant main effect since the *p*-values are less than 0.05. The Tests of Within-Subjects Contrasts show a significant linear effect since the *p*-value is less than 0.05 (<0.001). The Between-Subject Effects are not significant ($F(1,165) = 0.132$, $p = 0.717$). There is not a significant difference in between-groups means, since the *p*-values are more than 0.05 (0.122, 0.740, 0.350). Thus, H6 is supported for the haptic manipulations. In this case, a significant difference in the within-subjects groups is found only for the rough packaging with the baseline and the smooth one in PR, while the other *p*-values are more than 0.05.

Figure 7.6 presents the means and standard deviations results.

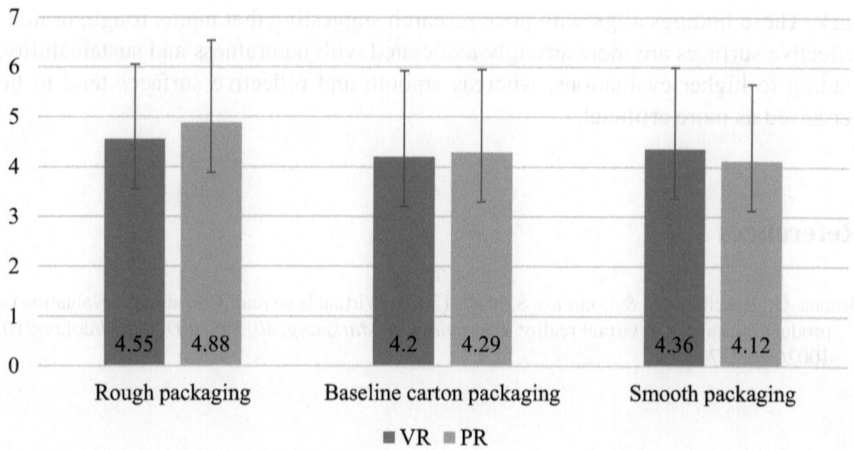

Fig. 7.6 Haptic cues, attractiveness

7.2 Discussion

Interesting discussion points emerge from the analysis of haptic packaging cues (rough pack, normal pack, smooth pack) across VR and PR, extending Branca et al. (2023).

First, results confirm a general alignment in consumer evaluations of haptic cues across VR and PR. Most dependent variables did not exhibit statistically significant differences between the two environments. Minor differences were identified only for the smooth packaging PS and ATP. The findings reinforce the robustness of VR as a platform for studying haptic-related packaging cues, despite the inherent absence of actual tactile feedback in virtual settings. This suggests that visual simulation of texture in VR can approximate real-world perception to a reasonable degree.

Second, while the overall pattern was stable, slight differences in magnitude emerged for specific manipulations. The rough packaging was generally rated higher in PR than in VR. This small discrepancy may reflect the fact that in physical settings, roughness is confirmed by tactile exploration, whereas in VR it can only be inferred visually, possibly reducing its salience or credibility. Conversely, the smooth packaging received slightly more favorable ratings in VR. Despite being cardboard, the reflective and glossy effect could have been stronger in the PR, although the dynamic light in VR produces an equally valid effect and the manipulation was properly perceived by the participants. Probably, touching the real smooth packaging with the hand triggers a more negative evaluation by consumers, compared to the counterpart in VR. However, this pattern seems also to align with Study 1, since the preference structure remained stable, while the evaluations were less polarized in VR.

Third, within-subject comparisons show that the rough packaging was consistently preferred and rated more positively across dimensions compared to the smooth pack. These findings align with prior research suggesting that matte, rough, or non-reflective surfaces are more strongly associated with naturalness and sustainability, leading to higher evaluations, whereas smooth and reflective surfaces tend to be perceived as more artificial.

References

Branca, G., Resciniti, R., & Loureiro, S. M. C. (2023). Virtual is so real! Consumers' evaluation of product packaging in virtual reality. *Psychology & Marketing, 40*, 596–609. https://doi.org/10.1002/mar.21743

Chapter 8
Study 3—Consumers' Response to Visual Cues

8.1 Study 3 Results

8.1.1 Perceived Sustainability

The green packaging is perceived to be the most sustainable among the alternatives in both treatments (VR: $M_{VRgreen} = 4.78$, $SD_{VRgreen} = 1.37$; PR: $M_{PRgreen} = 4.75$, $SD_{PRgreen} = 1.61$), followed by the baseline packaging in PR condition (VR: $M_{PRbaseline} = 4.68$, $SD_{PRbaseline} = 1.62$; PR: $M_{PRbeige} = 4.52$, $SD_{PRbeige} = 1.54$), and by the beige packaging in VR (VR: $M_{VRbeige} = 4.74$, $SD_{VRbeige} = 1.56$; VR: $M_{VRbaseline} = 4.60$, $SD_{VRbaseline} = 1.63$). Thus, H-PS3 is partially supported in the PR condition and supported in the VR condition.

Levene's Test of Equality of Error Variances shows *p*-values more than 0.05 (0.067, 0.607, 0.933). Mauchly's Test of Sphericity shows a *p*-value less than 0.05 (0.006). Interpreting the Greenhouse–Geisser corrected analysis and the Huynh–Feldt ($p = 0.259$) in the Tests of Within-Subjects Effects, there is no evidence of a significant main effect, because the *p*-values are more than 0.05. The Tests of Within-Subjects Contrasts do not show a significant linear effect since the *p*-value is more than 0.05 (0.171). The Between-Subject Effect is found to be not significant ($F(1,165) = 0.065$, $p = 0.799$). There is not a significant difference in between-groups means, since the *p*-values are more than 0.05 (0.888, 0.753, 0.374). Thus, H1 is supported also for the visual manipulations. There is not a significant difference in the within-subjects groups, since for all the manipulations the *p*-values are more than 0.05.

Figure 8.1 presents the means and standard deviations results.

G. Branca, *Virtual Reality, Real Intentions*, International Series in Advanced Management Studies, https://doi.org/10.1007/978-3-032-10142-6_8

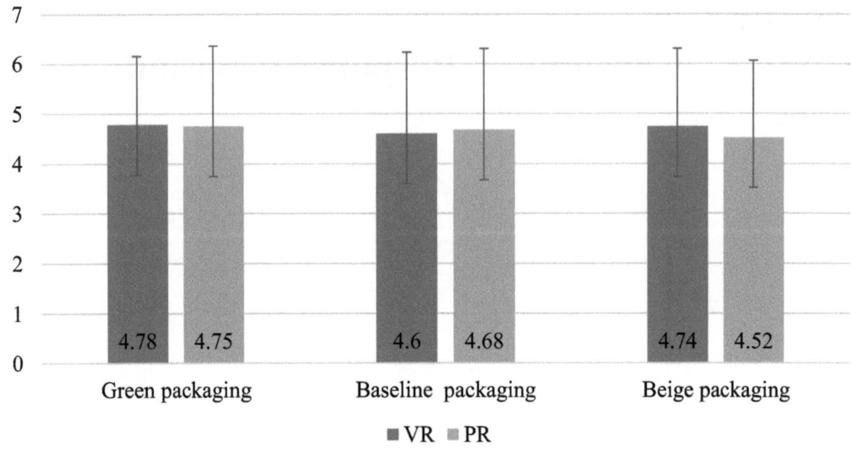

Fig. 8.1 Visual cues, perceived sustainability

8.1.2 Willingness to Pay a Premium Price

In VR, the green packaging shows the highest WTPP ($M_{VRgreen} = 3.93$, $SD_{VRgreen} = 1.60$), followed by the beige one ($M_{VRbeige} = 3.89$, $SD_{VRbeige} = 1.64$) and the baseline one ($M_{VRbaseline} = 3.74$, $SD_{VRbaseline} = 1.58$). By contrast, in PR, the baseline packaging shows the highest WTPP ($M_{PRbaseline} = 3.95$, $SD_{PRbaseline} = 1.60$), followed by the green one ($M_{PRgreen} = 3.86$, $SD_{PRgreen} = 1.66$) and beige one ($M_{PRbeige} = 3.73$, $SD_{PRbeige} = 1.54$). In this case, H-WTPP3 is supported in the VR condition and not supported in the PR condition.

Levene's Test of Equality of Error Variances shows *p*-values more than 0.05 (0.702, 0.775, 0.703). Mauchly's Test of Sphericity shows a *p*-value of more than 0.05 (0.817). Looking at the Multivariate Tests, there is no evidence of a significant main effect, since the *p*-values are more than 0.05. The Tests of Within-Subjects Contrasts do not show a significant linear effect since the *p*-value is more than 0.05 (0.389). The Between-Subject Effect is found to be not significant ($F(1,165) = 0.001$, $p = 0.980$). There is not a significant difference in between-groups means, since the *p*-values are more than 0.05 (0.772, 0.386, 0.523). Thus, H2 is supported also for the visual manipulations. There is not a significant difference in the within-subjects groups, since for all the manipulations the *p*-values are more than 0.05.

Figure 8.2 presents the means and standard deviations results.

8.1.3 Purchase Intention

The green packaging scored a similar PI in VR ($M_{VRgreen} = 4.15$, $SD_{VRgreen} = 1.60$) and in PR ($M_{PRgreen} = 3.98$, $SD_{PRgreen} = 1.58$). The baseline blue packaging scored

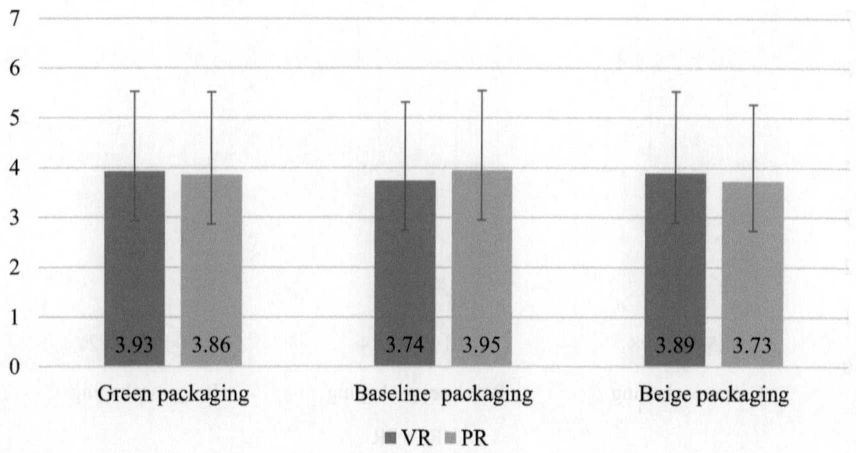

Fig. 8.2 Visual cues, willingness to pay a premium price

similar PI in VR ($M_{VRbaseline}$ = 4.10, $SD_{VRbaseline}$ = 1.52) and in PR ($M_{PRbaseline}$ = 4.14, $SD_{PRbaseline}$ = 1.45). The same happened for the beige packaging in VR ($M_{VRbeige}$ = 4.04, $SD_{VRbeige}$ = 1.66) and PR ($M_{PRbeige}$ = 3.82, $SD_{PRbeige}$ = 1.59). However, H-PI3 is partially supported in the VR condition and not supported in the PR condition.

Levene's Test of Equality of Error Variances shows *p*-values more than 0.05 (0.706, 0.407, 0.626). Mauchly's Test of Sphericity shows a *p*-value less than 0.05 (0.020). Interpreting the Greenhouse–Geisser corrected analysis and the Huynh–Feldt ($p = 0.162, 0.161$) in the Tests of Within-Subjects Effects, there is no evidence of a significant main effect because the *p*-values are more than 0.05. The Tests of Within-Subjects Contrasts do not show a significant linear effect since the *p*-value is more than 0.05 (0.207). The Between-Subject Effects are found to be not significant ($F(1,165) = 0.297$, $p = 0.586$). There is not a significant difference in between-groups means, since the *p*-values are more than 0.05 (0.499, 0.871, 0.391). Thus, H3 is supported also for the visual manipulations. There is not a significant difference in the within-subjects groups, since for all the manipulations the *p*-values are more than 0.05.

Figure 8.3 presents the means and standard deviations results.

8.1.4 Attitude Toward Packaging

The green packaging shows similar ATP in VR ($M_{VRgreen}$ = 4.56, $SD_{VRgreen}$ = 1.69) and in PR ($M_{PRgreen}$ = 4.43, $SD_{PRgreen}$ = 1.60). The baseline packaging scored similar ATP in VR ($M_{VRbaseline}$ = 4.42, $SD_{VRbaseline}$ = 1.58) and in PR ($M_{PRbaseline}$ = 4.61, $SD_{PRbaseline}$ = 1.43). The same happened for the beige packaging in VR ($M_{VRbeige}$

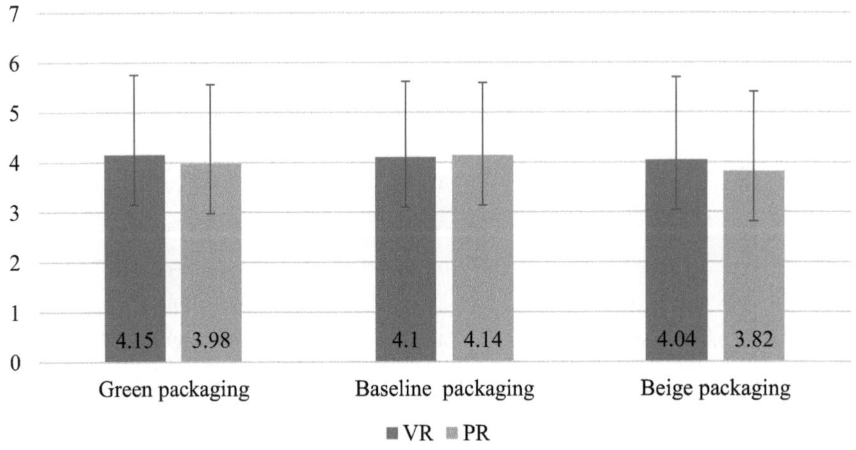

Fig. 8.3 Visual cues, purchase intention

$= 4.35$, $SD_{VRbeige} = 1.81$) and in PR ($M_{PRbeige} = 4.16$, $SD_{PRbeige} = 1.68$). However, H-ATP3 is only partially supported in both conditions.

Levene's Test of Equality of Error Variances shows *p*-values more than 0.05 for the green packaging (0.570) and the beige one (0.327), while the baseline one is slightly lower than 0.05 (0.042). Mauchly's Test of Sphericity shows a *p*-value of more than 0.05 (0.222). Looking at the Multivariate Tests, there is evidence of a significant main effect for the within-subject condition (0.05), while the *p*-value for the interaction is more than 0.05 (0.181). The Tests of Within-Subjects Contrasts show a significant linear effect since the *p*-value is less than 0.05 (0.033). The Between-Subject Effects are found to be not significant ($F(1,165) = 0.032, p = 0.858$). There is not a significant difference in between-groups means, since the *p*-values are more than 0.05 (0.622, 0.397, 0.486). Thus, H4 is supported also for the visual manipulations. There is not a significant difference in the within-subjects groups, since for all the manipulations the *p*-values are more than 0.05, except for the baseline packaging and the beige one in PR (0.020).

Figure 8.4 presents the means and standard deviations results.

8.1.5 *Perceived Quality*

The green packaging elicits similar PQ in VR ($M_{VRgreen} = 4.51$, $SD_{VRgreen} = 1.51$) and in PR ($M_{PRgreen} = 4.55$, $SD_{PRgreen} = 1.55$). The baseline packaging scored similar PQ in VR ($M_{VRbaseline} = 4.46$, $SD_{VRbaseline} = 1.48$) and in PR ($M_{PRbaseline} = 4.55$, $SD_{PRbaseline} = 1.46$). The same happened for the beige packaging in VR ($M_{VRbeige} = 4.39$, $SD_{VRbeige} = 1.67$) and in PR ($M_{PRbeige} = 4.29$, $SD_{PRbeige} = 1.60$). However, H-PQ3 is only partially supported in both conditions.

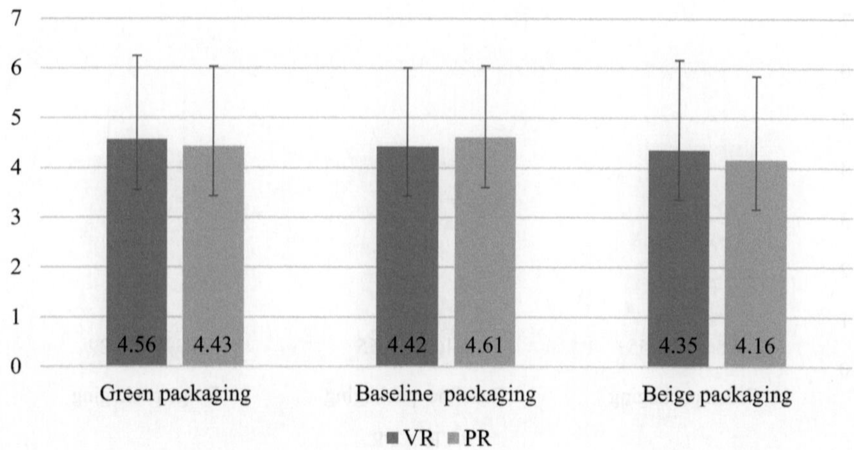

Fig. 8.4 Visual cues, attitude toward packaging

Levene's Test of Equality of Error Variances shows *p*-values more than 0.05 (0.878, 0.623, 0.517). Mauchly's Test of Sphericity shows a *p*-value of more than 0.05 (0.572). Looking at the Multivariate Tests, there is no evidence of a significant main effect since the *p*-values are more than 0.05 (0.153, 0.628). The Tests of Within-Subjects Contrasts do not show a significant linear effect since the *p*-value is more than 0.05 (0.08). The Between-Subject Effects are not significant ($F(1,165) = 0.002$, $p = 0.963$). There is not a significant difference in between-groups means, since the *p*-values are more than 0.05 (0.858, 0.693, 0.683). Thus, H5 is supported also for the visual manipulations. There is not a significant difference in the within-subjects groups, since for all the manipulations the *p*-values are more than 0.05.

Figure 8.5 presents the means and standard deviations results.

8.1.6 Attractiveness

The green packaging results in ATT in VR ($M_{VRgreen} = 4.24$, $SD_{VRgreen} = 1.75$) and in PR ($M_{PRgreen} = 4.14$, $SD_{PRgreen} = 1.61$). The baseline packaging scored similar ATT in VR ($M_{VRbaseline} = 4.20$, $SD_{VRbaseline} = 1.72$) and in PR ($M_{PRbaseline} = 4.29$, $SD_{PRbaseline} = 1.66$). The same happened for the beige packaging in VR ($M_{VRbeige} = 3.90$, $SD_{VRbeige} = 2.00$) and in PR ($M_{PRbeige} = 3.87$, $SD_{PRbeige} = 1.80$). However, H-ATT3 is partially supported in the VR condition and not supported in the PR condition.

Levene's Test of Equality of Error Variances shows *p*-values more than 0.05 (0.405, 0.483, 0.442). Mauchly's Test of Sphericity shows a *p*-value of more than 0.05 (0.99). Looking at the Multivariate Tests, there is evidence of a significant main effect for the within-subject condition (0.035), while the *p*-value for the interaction

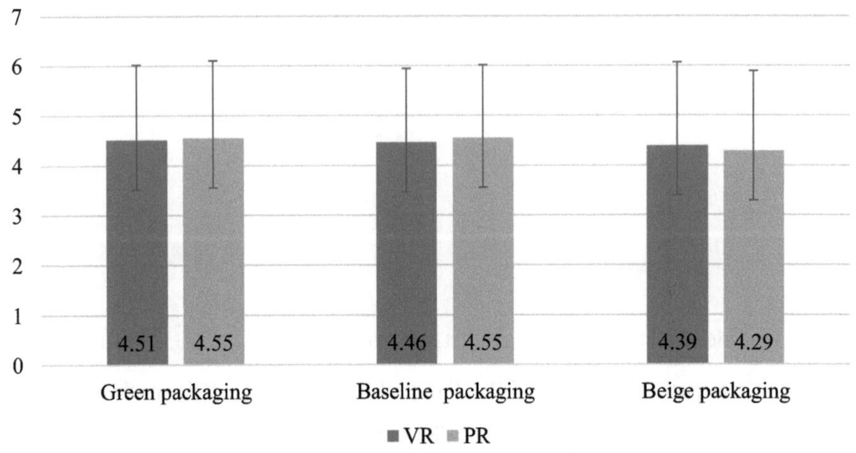

Fig. 8.5 Visual cues, perceived quality

is more than 0.05 (0.764). The Tests of Within-Subjects Contrasts show a significant linear effect since the *p*-value is less than 0.05 (0.033). The Between-Subject Effects are found to be not significant ($F(1,165) = 0.002, p = 0.962$). There is not a significant difference in between-groups means, since the *p*-values are more than 0.05 (0.719, 0.740, 0.932). Thus, H6 is supported also for the visual manipulations. There is not a significant difference in the within-subjects groups, since for all the manipulations the *p*-values are more than 0.05.

Figure 8.6 presents the means and standard deviations results.

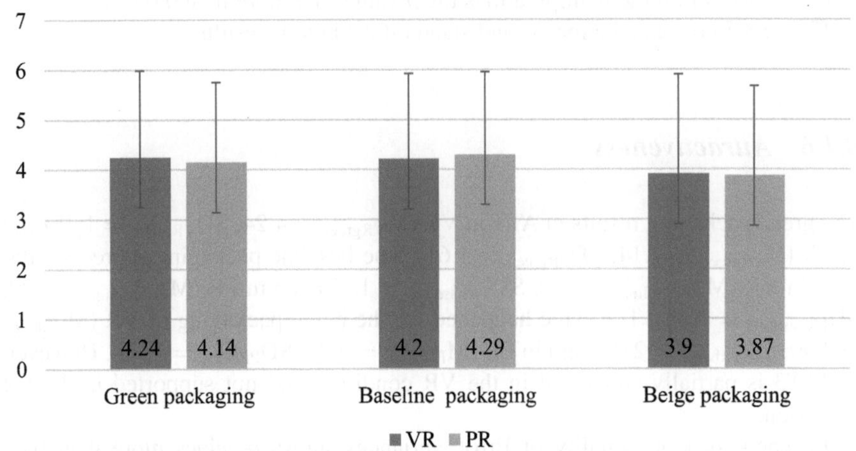

Fig. 8.6 Visual cues, attractiveness

8.2 Discussion

Study 3 provides interesting insight into the visual cues (green pack, beige pack, blue pack) assessment across VR and PR.

First, the results confirm a general consistency in consumer evaluations across VR and PR, with no statistically significant differences. This is not surprising, since visual cues should provide the highest level of similarity between the two conditions.

Second, the assumptions regarding packaging manipulations, however, are only partially supported or not supported at all. It does not emerge any statistically relevant difference in most of the within-subject treatments. Color does not seem to have an impact on consumer response, i.e., consumers do not seem to consider color relevant in their choices regarding packaging.

Chapter 9
Discussions, Implications, and Limitations of the Research

9.1 General Discussion

Some main aspects deserve to be further discussed.

First, the hypotheses of this research are supported in most cases. An overview is presented in Tables 9.1 and 9.2.

Building on Branca et al. (2023), results of Study 1 suggest that there seem to be no statistically significant differences between the consumers' evaluation of packaging in VR and PR when it comes to structural manipulations. Minor differences can be identified for the glass bottle PS and ATP between the two conditions. Similarly, in Study 2 no statistically significant differences emerged among all the variables in VR and PR when it comes to haptic manipulations, except for smooth packaging PS and ATP. Finally, in Study 3, there does not seem to be any statistically significant differences between the consumers' evaluation of packaging with color manipulations, in VR and PR, across all the measurements. Minor differences aside, it can be deduced that consumer response to packaging is consistent in VR and PR, considering different types of manipulation. This evidence extends previous literature on VR and consumer behavior, highlighting differences and similarities with PR (e.g., Branca et al., 2024; Branca et al., 2023; Cowan et al., 2021; Kim et al., 2021; Naderi et al., 2020; Peukert et al., 2019; Pfeiffer et al., 2020; Schnack et al., 2020; Siegrist et al., 2019).

Second, considering the results of the within-subjects groups, the effectiveness of different packaging manipulations could be defined. Frequently, variations in the material (Study 1) have shown a significant impact on the consumers' response. This is in line with previous research, which claims that consumers use packaging material as a cue to assess the packaging and the product (e.g., Chrysochou & Festila, 2019; Festila & Chrysochou, 2018; Nguyen et al., 2020). The influence of packaging manipulations is weaker in Study 2, since the cases in which there is no statistically significant difference within haptic cues are more frequent than in Study 1. This

G. Branca, *Virtual Reality, Real Intentions*, International Series in Advanced Management Studies, https://doi.org/10.1007/978-3-032-10142-6_9

Table 9.1 Summary of high-order hypotheses and results

Hypothesis	Study	Manipulations	Significant difference between VR and PR	Results
H1	1	Glass bottle Baseline packaging Plastic bottle	√	Partially supported
	2	Rough packaging Baseline packaging Smooth packaging	√	Partially supported
	3	Green packaging Baseline packaging Beige packaging		Supported
H2	1	Glass bottle Baseline packaging Plastic bottle		Supported
	2	Rough packaging Baseline packaging Smooth packaging		Supported
	3	Green packaging Baseline packaging Beige packaging		Supported
H3	1	Glass bottle Baseline packaging Plastic bottle		Supported
	2	Rough packaging Baseline packaging Smooth packaging		Supported
	3	Green packaging Baseline packaging Beige packaging		Supported
H4	1	Glass bottle Baseline packaging Plastic bottle	√	Partially supported
	2	Rough packaging Baseline packaging Smooth packaging	√	Partially supported
	3	Green packaging Baseline packaging Beige packaging		Supported
H5	1	Glass bottle Baseline packaging Plastic bottle		Supported
	2	Rough packaging Baseline packaging Smooth packaging		Supported

(continued)

Table 9.1 (continued)

Hypothesis	Study	Manipulations	Significant difference between VR and PR	Results
	3	Green packaging Baseline packaging Beige packaging		Supported
H6	1	Glass bottle Baseline packaging Plastic bottle		Supported
	2	Rough packaging Baseline packaging Smooth packaging		Supported
	3	Green packaging Baseline packaging Beige packaging		Supported

Table 9.2 Summary of low-order hypotheses and results

Study	Hypothesis	Results in VR	Results in PR
1	H-PS1	Supported	Supported
	H-WTPP1	Supported	Supported
	H-PI1	Supported	Supported
	H-ATP1	Supported	Supported
	H-PQ1	Supported	Supported
	H-ATT1	Supported	Supported
2	H-PS2	Supported	Supported
	H-WTPP2	Partially supported	Supported
	H-PI2	Partially supported	Supported
	H-ATP2	Partially supported	Supported
	H-PQ2	Partially supported	Supported
	H-ATT2	Partially supported	Supported
3	H-PS3	Supported	Partially supported
	H-WTPP3	Supported	Not supported
	H-PI3	Partially supported	Not supported
	H-ATP3	Partially supported	Partially supported
	H-PQ3	Partially supported	Partially supported
	H-ATT3	Partially supported	Not supported

extends previous literature, which found haptic cues to influence consumers' evaluation (e.g., Chen, 2021; Karana, 2012; Karana & Nijkamp, 2014). Interestingly, color does not seem to have an impact on consumer response: in almost no case the differences within manipulations of Study 3 are significant. In this context, consumers do not seem to consider color relevant in their choices regarding packaging. This result contrasts with previous literature since color was found effective in shaping consumers' evaluation (e.g., Chrysochou & Festila, 2019; Festila & Chrysochou, 2018; Marozzo et al., 2020).

Third, the range between the highest- and lowest-rated packaging alternatives is generally narrower in VR than in PR. This suggests that participants' evaluations tend to be less extreme in virtual environments, possibly due to the reduced availability of certain sensory cues (e.g., touch, weight). This finding extends the results of Branca et al. (2023), indicating that although VR effectively captures relative preferences among packaging alternatives, it may temper strong attitudinal reactions (both positive and negative) compared to physical settings.

Fourth, when examining the results of the studies concurrently, it is possible to observe how the glass bottle and the rough packaging always generate the highest scores, in both conditions. Likewise, plastic bottles always generate the most negative response from consumers. This result is probably a consequence of the perceived superior sustainability of the glass (Boesen et al., 2019; Steenis et al., 2017), and the rough texture, which can recall naturalness (Karana, 2012). As pointed out by several authors, consumers often rely on the material, rather than other packaging features, to assess its eco-friendliness, regardless of the actual sustainability (e.g., Herbes et al., 2020; Nguyen et al., 2020). In this line, packaging perceived sustainability across the three studies shows results with higher deviations within the alternatives for the structural cues, while the variations within the manipulations of haptic cues are smaller, and visual cues are even more reduced. Probably individuals, while recognizing differences in mock-ups in different studies, rely more on the packaging material than on the haptic response, and even less on color when it comes to sustainability, regardless of the experimental condition. Similar findings are shown for the other attitudinal measures.

9.2 Theoretical Implications

This study intends to contribute to the literature on VR and packaging in at least four ways.

First, by contrasting consumers' evaluation of packaging in VR and PR, it is clarified how the two conditions are consistent in terms of consumer response. Regardless of whether individuals are evaluating virtual or physical packaging, its cues are salient to them. Moreover, VR leads to the same outcomes as PR in terms of attitudes, intentions, and perceptions, aside from minor differences. This result addresses previous literature, calling for more research about consumer behavior and product evaluation in VR and differences with physical products (e.g., Branca et al., 2023; Cowan et al., 2021; Kim et al., 2021; Pfeiffer et al., 2020). Furthermore, it extends recent studies, focusing on a specific attribute of the product, i.e., packaging, and manipulating its features, following an atomistic approach (e.g., Branca et al., 2024; Huang et al., 2021; Naderi et al., 2020; Peukert et al., 2019; Schnack et al., 2020; Siegrist et al., 2019). Finally, it addresses little consensus on consumers' responses to VR and some mixed findings that emerged in previous literature, highlighting the similarities between outcomes in VR and PR (e.g., Cowan et al., 2021; Kang et al., 2020; Martínez-Navarro et al., 2019; Meißner et al., 2020; Mishra et al., 2021; Park & Kim, 2021; Wedel et al., 2020; Xi & Hamari, 2021).

Second, this research leverages the features of VR for conducting packaging and product research. Unlike previous literature, which generally employed 2D images in their studies (e.g., Herédia-Colaço, 2023; Machiels & Orth, 2017; Orth & Crouch, 2014; Park & Ma, 2019; Qiao & Griffin, 2022), here physical packaging in PR and realistic 3D stimuli in VR were employed, obtaining similar results in the two conditions. This is of particular interest to researchers as it corroborates previous literature, according to which VR is a suitable environment for consumer and product research, which elicits realistic behavior, reduces external variable influence, generates high experiential control and ecological validity, and overcomes the limitations of laboratory and traditional studies (Bernritter et al., 2021; Harz et al., 2021; Huang et al., 2021; Meißner et al., 2020; Schnack et al., 2020). We echo Zhang et al. (2025), who highlight the need for VR to move beyond entertainment and offer value in enhancing product understanding and evaluation, with product diagnosticity being crucial in purchase decisions.

Third, the results of this study are particularly interesting for packaging structural and haptic manipulations. In fact, although in VR it is not possible to physically touch materials and textures, consumers perceived cues as intended. This is in line with Alzayat and Lee (2021), who state that VR can simulate real products and allow consumers to haptically explore them. Inducing haptic perception in consumers is particularly relevant for online shopping (Briand Decré & Cloonan, 2019). The research echoes Littel and Orth (2013), who claim that consumer evaluation is impacted by the presence of packaging haptic features, especially when these attributes are semantically congruent with visuals. Similarly, it extends Briand Decré and Cloonan (2019), according to which the visual sense is well-suited for assessing material or haptic properties, highlighting the potential of VR in this context. Indeed, a critical factor for consumers when shopping online is the desire to examine a product before making a purchase (Briand Decré & Cloonan, 2019). Following Holmes and Paswan (2012), the more direct experience the consumers have through as many senses as possible, the more informed judgment they can have about a product. VR proved to be a suitable environment for a direct and complete packaging evaluation, generating overlapping results with PR.

Finally, this research contributes to the knowledge about packaging cues' effectiveness in shaping consumers' responses, following an analytical approach (Chrysochou & Festila, 2019) and extending previous literature (e.g., Festila & Chrysochou, 2018; Herbes et al., 2020; Herédia-Colaço, 2023; Magnier & Crié, 2015). Packaging can influence attitudes and intentions through its design elements (Chen, 2021; Coelho do Vale & Verga Matos, 2015; Park & Ma, 2019). However, this research shows that not all packaging attributes are equally effective. The results imply that packaging material is the most relevant attribute in influencing consumer choice (Boesen et al., 2019; Festila & Chrysochou, 2018; Herbes et al., 2020; Nguyen et al., 2020; Steenis et al., 2017), followed by packaging texture (Chen, 2021; Karana,

2012; Karana & Nijkamp, 2014). Unlike some of the previous literature (e.g., Chrysochou & Festila, 2019; Festila & Chrysochou, 2018; Marozzo et al., 2020), color does not seem to be a relevant factor in consumer choice in this context or, at least, is less important than the other attributes considered in this research. Building on the cue utilization theory (Olson, 1978), the research highlights the potential of the analytical approach in providing a comprehensive understanding of consumer responses to different packaging cues, by analyzing them in isolation.

9.3 Managerial Contributions

This research intends to provide at least three recommendations for managers, retailers, packaging designers, and marketing practitioners. The findings highlight how VR can be effectively employed as a decision-support tool to prototype, test, and refine product-packaging designs, particularly sustainable solutions, before committing to large-scale production, as well as in shopping environments.

First, VR and PR exhibit similar patterns in terms of consumer responses, suggesting that VR can effectively serve as a consumption environment and for conducting product evaluations and packaging tests. Managers and practitioners can find value in this research as VR has the potential to revolutionize various aspects of product development, including design, prototyping, and consumer evaluation (Bu et al., 2021; Huang et al., 2021; Hube et al., 2020). Traditional product and packaging tests have long grappled with issues related to cost, time, and flexibility, stemming from the need for physical mock-ups and the challenges of effecting rapid model changes. Here, VR presents an agile solution with clear advantages (such as performing tests without the use of physical mock-ups, the possibility and immediacy of carrying out or presenting variations of the same model, allowing more data and information from the test), leading to a more efficient, resource-friendly, and time-effective process leading to PR-like results. Indeed, this positions VR as a practical instrument for integrating innovation processes with sustainability goals: virtual prototyping reduces material waste, energy consumption, and the environmental impact associated with repeated physical iterations. Moreover, immersive VR allows global and multi-market testing without the logistical complexity of shipping prototypes, making it a strategic asset for firms operating across international markets or pursuing rapid packaging innovation cycles.

Second, this research offers valuable insight into consumer behavior dynamics within VR environments and virtual packaging evaluations. This knowledge equips businesses to craft effective product strategies in VR, acknowledging that consumers can discern specific stimuli and perceive distinctions among different alternatives, even in the absence of physical interaction with the products. VR proves to be an effective platform for manipulating packaging cues, including materials, textures, and colors. As highlighted in previous literature (Fares et al., 2024), VR offers businesses cost-effective experiential marketing opportunities, stronger emotional connections, and greater customer engagement and enjoyment, compared to other media. VR achieves this through high sensory breadth, i.e., multiple sensory cues like audio and video, and sensory depth, delivering high-quality and realistic content. This immersive experience elevates media richness, prompting marketers to explore effective strategies to leverage VR for optimizing consumer experiences. Moreover, the integration of realistic environmental contexts (e.g., retail shelves, digital store simulations) can enable managers to evaluate not only product-level reactions but also broader shopping behaviors, attention patterns, and engagement with specific products' attributes, e.g., sustainability cues.

Third, practitioners should recognize that consumers exhibit a greater reliance on the material of the packaging over haptic cues. Moreover, packaging color manipulations did not prove to be effective in shaping consumers' attitudes and intentions in this context. Based on this, it is possible to define effective packaging design strategies that can support determining a product's success and help brands differentiate from competitors, while accounting for the sustainability goals. This evidence suggests a shift of focus toward material authenticity and structural elements rather than aesthetic features alone. In addition, VR provides a controlled testing ground for eco-friendly materials and textures perception, allowing companies to estimate attitudes and perceptions for sustainable packaging before committing resources to large-scale changes. These insights are not only relevant for design and branding teams but also for supply chain and sustainability managers, who can leverage VR results to support investments in sustainable packaging innovation while reducing development costs. Furthermore, the results offer policy-relevant guidance, as they demonstrate how immersive evaluation methods can support industry compliance with sustainability regulations and voluntary efforts.

9.4 Limitations and Recommendations for Future Research

Although this research aims to offer valuable implications for researchers and practitioners, it has some limitations that should be addressed.

The results' generalizability may be affected, since all the participants were Italian consumers, identified by convenience sampling. Future research should consider a larger sample within a multicultural context to enhance external validity (Mishra et al., 2021).

Providing realistic stimuli in the experimental procedure has been a priority. However, echoing Park and Ma (2019), laboratory experiments allow researchers to gain advantages in uniformity of procedures, variable manipulations, control of external variables and internal validity, while they have limited external validity in reflecting actual behavior and real decision-making environment. Future studies should therefore complement controlled experiments with field settings or hybrid designs to validate the robustness of findings.

A single product category was employed to test packaging manipulation. However, even if the product category should not have an influence on the results, in line with Liao et al. (2015), some bias may exist from specific product knowledge, when it comes to the packaging attributes such as colors and materials. While the present study focused on grocery products, future research should explore categories with greater symbolic value, involvement, and purchase complexity. VR offers unique opportunities to expand research boundaries, enabling studies that are not easily conducted in traditional settings.

This research employed no other technologies in addition to HMD. Next studies could integrate the experimentation using tools that track movements of the eyes or body, to understand more in-depth consumer behavior and take full advantage of the use of autonomous technologies in conducting experiments (Schnack et al., 2020, 2021; van Berlo et al., 2021). Moreover, similarly to previous literature on VR, this research analyzes consumers' attitudes, rather than actual behaviors, an issue that should be addressed in future studies, also to increase external validity (Viglia et al., 2021).

Another limitation of this research is that it focused on packaging materials, textures, and colors, while other packaging attributes were not addressed. Some elements, such as shape and weight, cannot yet be fully replicated in VR. This represents an important gap, as shape and weight may play a crucial role in consumer perception of quality, functionality, and sustainability. In addition, future studies could explore potential interactions among packaging cues themselves, which may influence consumer responses in more complex ways than isolated attributes.

Finally, this study does not cover all possible outcomes, nor does it account for the potential presence of moderating effects. While the analyses focused on attitudes, intentions, and perceptions, future research could extend the scope by including moderators that may influence the strength and direction of consumer responses in VR versus PR. Consumers' characteristics (e.g., product category involvement, sustainability orientation, familiarity with VR), contextual factors (e.g., retail setting), and technological aspects (e.g., degree of immersion, quality of VR simulation) could all shape how packaging cues are perceived and evaluated.

References

Alzayat, A., & Lee, S. H. M. (2021). Virtual products as an extension of my body: Exploring hedonic and utilitarian shopping value in a virtual reality retail environment. *Journal of Business Research, 130*, 348–363. https://doi.org/10.1016/j.jbusres.2021.03.017

Bernritter, S. F., Ketelaar, P. E., & Sotgiu, F. (2021). Behaviorally targeted location-based mobile marketing. *Journal of the Academy of Marketing Science, 49*, 677–702. https://doi.org/10.1007/s11747-021-00784-0

Boesen, S., Bey, N., & Niero, M. (2019). Environmental sustainability of liquid food packaging. Is there a gap between Danish consumers' perception and learnings from life cycle assessment? *Journal of Cleaner Production, 210*, 1193–1206. https://doi.org/10.1016/j.jclepro.2018.11.055

Branca, G., Marino, V., & Resciniti, R. (2024). How do consumers evaluate products in virtual reality? A literature review for a research agenda. *Spanish Journal of Marketing—ESIC, 28*(3), 356–380. https://doi.org/10.1108/SJME-07-2022-0153

Branca, G., Resciniti, R., & Loureiro, S. M. C. (2023). Virtual is so real! Consumers' evaluation of product packaging in virtual reality. *Psychology & Marketing, 40*, 596–609. https://doi.org/10.1002/mar.21743

Briand Decré, G., & Cloonan, C. (2019). A touch of gloss: Haptic perception of packaging and consumers' reactions. *Journal of Product & Brand Management, 28*(1), 117–132. https://doi.org/10.1108/JPBM-05-2017-1472

Bu, L., Chen, C. H., Ng, K. K. H., Zheng, P., Dong, G., & Liu, H. (2021). A user-centric design approach for smart product-service systems using virtual reality: A case study. *Journal of Cleaner Production, 280*(2), Article 124413. https://doi.org/10.1016/j.jclepro.2020.124413

Chen, Y. S. A. (2021). Does outward appearance appeal to the inward mind? The impact of packaging finishes on brand impressions and the subsequent behavior of consumer. *Journal of Product & Brand Management, 30*(5), 768–778. https://doi.org/10.1108/JPBM-07-2019-2466

Chrysochou, P., & Festila, A. (2019). A content analysis of organic product package designs. *Journal of Consumer Marketing, 36*(4), 441–448. https://doi.org/10.1108/JCM-06-2018-2720

Coelho do Vale, R., & Verga Matos, P. (2015). The impact of copycat packaging strategies on the adoption of private labels. *Journal of Product & Brand Management, 24*(6), 646–659. https://doi.org/10.1108/JPBM-03-2015-0846

Cowan, K., Spielmann, N., Horn, E., & Griffart, C. (2021). Perception is reality… How digital retail environments influence brand perceptions through presence. *Journal of Business Research, 123*, 86–96. https://doi.org/10.1016/j.jbusres.2020.09.058

Fares, O. H., Aversa, J., Lee, S. H., & Jacobson, J. (2024). Virtual reality: A review and a new framework for integrated adoption. *International Journal of Consumer Studies, 48*(2), Article e13040. https://doi.org/10.1111/ijcs.13040

Festila, A., & Chrysochou, P. (2018). Implicit communication of food product healthfulness through package design: A content analysis. *Journal of Consumer Behavior, 17*, 461–476. https://doi.org/10.1002/cb.1732

Harz, N., Hohenberg, S., & Homburg, C. (2021). Virtual Reality in New Product Development: insights from pre-launch sales forecasting for durables. *Journal of Marketing*, 1–23. https://doi.org/10.1177/00222429211014902

Herbes, C., Beuthner, C., & Ramme, I. (2020). How green is your packaging—A comparative international study of cues consumers use to recognize environmentally friendly packaging. *International Journal of Consumer Studies, 44*(3), 258–271. https://doi.org/10.1111/ijcs.12560

Herédia-Colaço, V. (2023). Pro-environmental messages have more effect when they come from less familiar brands. *Journal of Product & Brand Management, 32*(3), 436–453. https://doi.org/10.1108/JPBM-12-2021-3782

Holmes, G. R., & Paswan, A. (2012). Consumer reaction to new package design. *Journal of Product & Brand Management, 21*(2), 109–116. https://doi.org/10.1108/10610421211215553

Huang, J., Zhao, P., & Wan, X. (2021). From brain variations to individual differences in the color–flavor incongruency effect: A combined virtual reality and resting-state fMRI study. *Journal of Business Research, 123*, 604–612. https://doi.org/10.1016/j.jbusres.2020.10.031

Hube, N., Müller, M., Lapczyna, E., & Wojdziak, J. (2020). Mixed Reality based collaboration for design processes. *i-com, 19(2)*, 123–137. https://doi.org/10.1515/icom-2020-0012

Kang, H. J., Shin, J., & Ponto, K. (2020). How 3D Virtual Reality stores can shape consumer purchase decisions: The roles of informativeness and playfulness. *Journal of Interactive Marketing, 49*, 70–85. https://doi.org/10.1016/j.intmar.2019.07.002

Karana, E. (2012). Characterization of 'natural' and 'high-quality' materials to improve perception of bio-plastics. *Journal of Cleaner Production, 37*, 316–325. https://doi.org/10.1016/j.jclepro.2012.07.034

Karana, E., & Nijkamp, N. (2014). Fiberness, reflectiveness and roughness in the characterization of natural and high quality materials. *Journal of Cleaner Production, 68*, 252–260. https://doi.org/10.1016/j.jclepro.2014.01.001

Kim, J.-H., Kim, M., Park, M., & Yoo, J. (2021). How interactivity and vividness influence consumer virtual reality shopping experience: The mediating role of telepresence. *Journal of Research in Interactive Marketing, 15*(3), 502–525. https://doi.org/10.1108/JRIM-07-2020-0148

Liao, L. L., Corsi, A. M., Chrysochou, P., & Larry Lockshin, L. (2015). Emotional responses towards food packaging: A joint application of self-report and physiological measures of emotion. *Food Quality and Preference, 42*, 48–55. https://doi.org/10.1016/j.foodqual.2015.01.009

Littel, S., & Orth, U. R. (2013). Effects of package visuals and haptics on brand evaluations. *European Journal of Marketing, 47*(1/2), 198–217. https://doi.org/10.1108/03090561311285510

Machiels, C. J. A., & Orth, U. R. (2017). Verticality in product labels and shelves as a metaphorical cue to quality. *Journal of Retailing and Consumer Services, 37*, 195–203. https://doi.org/10.1016/j.jretconser.2017.02.009

Magnier, L., & Crié, D. (2015). Communicating packaging eco-friendliness: An exploration of consumers' perceptions of eco-designed packaging. *International Journal of Retail & Distribution Management, 43*(4/5), 350–366. https://doi.org/10.1108/IJRDM-04-2014-0048

Marozzo, V., Raimondo, M. A., Miceli, G. "Nino," & Scopelliti, I. (2020). Effects of au naturel packaging colors on willingness to pay for healthy food. *Psychology & Marketing, 37(7)*, 913–927. https://doi.org/10.1002/mar.21294

Martínez-Navarro, J., Bigné, E., Guixeres, J., Alcañiz, M., & Torrecilla, C. (2019). The influence of virtual reality in e-commerce. *Journal of Business Research, 100*, 475–482. https://doi.org/10.1016/j.jbusres.2018.10.054

Meißner, M., Pfeiffer, J., Peukert, C., Dietrich, H., & Pfeiffer, T. (2020). How virtual reality affects consumer choice. *Journal of Business Research, 117*, 219–231. https://doi.org/10.1016/j.jbusres.2020.06.004

Mishra, A., Shukla, A., Rana, N. P., & Dwivedi, Y. K. (2021). From "touch" to a "multisensory" experience: The impact of technology interface and product type on consumer responses. *Psychology & Marketing, 38*, 385–396. https://doi.org/10.1002/mar.21436

Naderi, E., Naderi, I., & Balakrishnan, B. (2020). Product design matters, but is it enough? Consumers' responses to product design and environment congruence. *Journal of Product & Brand Management, 29*(7), 939–954. https://doi.org/10.1108/JPBM-08-2018-1975

Nguyen, A. T., Parker, L., Brennan, L., & Lockrey, S. (2020). A consumer definition of eco-friendly packaging. *Journal of Cleaner Production, 252*, Article 119792. https://doi.org/10.1016/j.jclepro.2019.119792

Olson, J.C. (1978). Inferential Belief Formation in the Cue Utilization Process. In *Advances in Consumer Research Volume 05* (pp. 706–713). Association for Consumer Research. https://www.acrwebsite.org/volumes/9509/volumes/v05/NA-05

Orth, U. R., & Crouch, R. C. (2014). Is Beauty in the Aisles of the Retailer? Package Processing in Visually Complex Contexts. *Journal of Retailing, 90*(4), 524–537. https://doi.org/10.1016/j.jretai.2014.05.004

Park, H., & Kim, S. (2021). Do augmented and virtual reality technologies increase consumers' purchase intentions? The role of cognitive elaboration and shopping goals. *Clothing and Textiles Research Journal, 41*(2). https://doi.org/10.1177/0887302X21994287

Park, J., & Ma, Y. J. (2019). Number-location bias: Do consumers correctly process the number on the product package? *Journal of Product & Brand Management, 28*(1), 80–94. https://doi.org/10.1108/JPBM-12-2017-1711

Peukert, C., Pfeiffer, J., Meißner, M., Pfeiffer, T., & Weinhardt, C. (2019). Shopping in Virtual Reality stores: The influence of immersion on system adoption. *Journal of Management Information Systems, 36*(3), 755–788. https://doi.org/10.1080/07421222.2019.1628889

Pfeiffer, P., Pfeiffer, T., Meißner, M., & Weiß, E. (2020). Eye-Tracking-based classification of information search behavior using Machine Learning: Evidence from experiments in physical shops and Virtual Reality shopping environments. *Information Systems Research, 31*(3), 675–691. https://doi.org/10.1287/isre.2019.0907

Qiao, F., & Griffin, W. G. (2022). Brand imitation strategy, package design and consumer response: What does it take to make a difference? *Journal of Product & Brand Management, 31*(2), 177–188. https://doi.org/10.1108/JPBM-05-2019-2363

Schnack, A., Wright, M. J., & Elms, J. (2021). Investigating the impact of shopper personality on behaviour in immersive Virtual Reality store environments. *Journal of Retailing and Consumer Services, 61*, Article 102581. https://doi.org/10.1016/j.jretconser.2021.102581

Schnack, A., Wright, M. J., & Holdershaw, J. L. (2020). An exploratory investigation of shopper behaviour in an immersive virtual reality store. *Journal of Consumer Behaviour, 19*, 182–195. https://doi.org/10.1002/cb.1803

Siegrist, M., Ung, C.-Y., Zank, M., Marinello, M., Kunz, A., Hartmann, C., & Menozzi, M. (2019). Consumers' food selection behaviors in three-dimensional (3D) virtual reality. *Food Research International, 117*, 50–59. https://doi.org/10.1016/j.foodres.2018.02.033

Steenis, N. D., van Herpen, E., van der Lans, I. A., Ligthart, T. N., & van Trijp, H. C. M. (2017). Consumer response to packaging design. The role of packaging materials and graphics in sustainability perceptions and product evaluations. *Journal of Cleaner Production, 162*, 286–298. https://doi.org/10.1016/j.jclepro.2017.06.036

van Berlo, Z. M. C., van Reijmersdal, E. A., Smit, E. G., & van der Laan, L. N. (2021). Brands in virtual reality games: Affective processes within computer-mediated consumer experiences. *Journal of Business Research, 122*, 458–465. https://doi.org/10.1016/j.jbusres.2020.09.006

Viglia, G., Zaefarian, G., & Ulqinaku, A. (2021). How to design good experiments in marketing: Types, examples, and methods. *Industrial Marketing Management, 98*, 193–206. https://doi.org/10.1016/j.indmarman.2021.08.007

Wedel, M., Bigné, E., & Zhang, J. (2020). Virtual and augmented reality: Advancing research in consumer marketing. *International Journal of Research in Marketing, 37*(3), 443–465. https://doi.org/10.1016/j.ijresmar.2020.04.004

Xi, N., & Hamari, J. (2021). Shopping in virtual reality: A literature review and future agenda. *Journal of Business Research, 134*, 37–58. https://doi.org/10.1016/j.jbusres.2021.04.075

Zhang, Y., Shao, W., Quach, S., Thaichon, P., & Li, Q. (2025). VR retailing: When and why immersion pays off. *Journal of Retailing*. https://doi.org/10.1016/j.jretai.2025.04.004

Chapter 10
Conclusions

Conducted as part of a three-year Ph.D. project, this research contributes to advancing knowledge at the intersection of marketing, technology, and sustainability. This volume investigated how consumers evaluate packaged products in Virtual Reality (VR) compared to physical reality (PR), offering a comparative experimental analysis that addresses a relevant and timely gap in consumer research and marketing practice. Anchored in the dual importance of packaging design, both as a strategic marketing tool and a key driver of sustainable consumption, this research explored whether VR could elicit consumer evaluations of packaging as effectively as PR, thus supporting the use of immersive technologies in experimental marketing. In doing so, it emphasized how sustainability-oriented packaging attributes are tested and perceived across environments, highlighting VR's potential to advance sustainable innovation while reducing the environmental footprint of the process itself.

The work unfolded over several chapters. The introductory chapters reviewed two key domains: the role of VR in consumer and product research, and the literature on packaging design, sustainability, and consumer response. Specifically, chapter 2 positions VR as both an emerging consumer touchpoint and a valid research environment, highlighting its immersive and interactive capabilities, as well as its advantages compared to traditional experimental settings. Chapter 3 mainly discusses the analytical approaches to packaging design evaluation, with particular emphasis on sustainability cues, such as material, texture, and color, that served as the basis for the experimental manipulations in this research.

Building on this foundation, Chap. 4 defines the research questions and hypotheses, outlining a methodological approach consisting of a qualitative preliminary study and three experimental studies, while Chap. 5 presents the methodological setup and procedures. Chapters 6, 7, and 8 each focused on a specific packaging cue, respectively structural (glass vs. carton vs. plastic), haptic (rough vs. regular vs. smooth), and visual (green vs. beige vs. blue), and reported findings on six key dependent variables measuring attitudes and intentions. Across the three experiments, results showed substantial consistency between evaluations made in VR and PR.

G. Branca, *Virtual Reality, Real Intentions*, International Series in Advanced Management Studies, https://doi.org/10.1007/978-3-032-10142-6_10

While some minor differences emerged, consumer responses across environments were largely aligned. Importantly, the immersive nature of VR was appropriate to elicit complex attitudinal and behavioral responses, supporting its role as a viable alternative to traditional experimental settings for packaging evaluation and as a novel shopping environment. The findings also confirmed that perceived sustainable packaging materials and texture are consistently perceived as better options, underscoring their strategic importance for firms pursuing eco-friendly positioning, while showing that color manipulations were less effective.

Chapter 9 synthesized these findings, offering theoretical contributions to the literature on immersive consumer research, practical implications for marketers and product developers, and methodological guidance for future research using VR. The results indicate that, under appropriate conditions, VR can serve not only as a test environment for packaging design but also as a space where consumers construct meaningful product evaluations. From a sustainability perspective, this means VR enables firms to test and refine packaging solutions before moving to resource-intensive physical production, thus aligning product development with sustainability principles. This opens promising avenues for using VR in the early phases of product and packaging development, prototyping, and consumer testing, particularly for categories such as FMCGs, where packaging is central to brand perception and choice. Ultimately, this work confirms the potential of VR not only as a tool for innovative marketing practice but also as a robust method for academic research into consumer behavior, bridging technological innovation with the pressing need for sustainable consumption and production.

MIX
Papier aus verantwortungsvollen Quellen
Paper from responsible sources
FSC® C105338

If you have any concerns about our products,
you can contact us on
ProductSafety@springernature.com

In case Publisher is established outside the EU,
the EU authorized representative is:
Springer Nature Customer Service Center GmbH
Europaplatz 3, 69115 Heidelberg, Germany

Printed by Libri Plureos GmbH
in Hamburg, Germany